THE
ENGLISH
INHERITANCE

THE
ENGLISH
INHERITANCE

An Historical Essay

G. KITSON CLARK
Fellow of Trinity College
Cambridge

S C M PRESS LTD
56 Bloomsbury Street, London WC1

First published 1950

*Printed in Great Britain by The Camelot Press Ltd.,
London and Southampton*

TO
CHARLES SMYTH
IN MEMORY OF MANY WALKS AND TALKS AT
CAMBRIDGE

CONTENTS

INTRODUCTION

THIS book is intended to be an essay on the effects of the Christian religion on the English inheritance. Any work on so vast a subject must be inadequate, and how inadequate is mine has been suggested to me by several unhappy moments after I had surrendered my typescript to the publishers beyond the possibility of additions. But I put the book forward in the same belief as that in which I accepted the task when it was first suggested to me. The subject is so urgently important that anything which sets minds to work upon it will be of value. However, in order to do this satisfactorily, it is important to set to work systematically, and it is probably desirable to say here how I have defined my task, and in particular, to make it clear what I have not tried to do. I have not tried to rival those excellent books which appear from time to time on the 'English Spirit' or the 'English Tradition'. Such books necessarily deal with imponderables and must try to generalize about the whole field. I do not for a moment intend to underrate their importance, but it seemed to me to be desirable in this work to try to get down to some of the bones of the subject and to deal with certain particular traditions, habits or arrangements which have historical antecedents, and to describe those antecedents. The elements I have selected as being of chief importance are the rule of law, the belief in freedom, the sense of personal responsibility, and the belief in religious toleration; and I have endeavoured to trace their roots and to examine their growth at certain points in English history. This method is necessarily eclectic, but it seems to be better for present purposes, better as a starting point for clear thought and discussion, to do this than to attempt a series of generalizations which might more comprehensively cover the whole field.

In order to pursue this method I have had to use a good deal of history, but I have not tried to write a new history of England. I have necessarily chosen and summarized my history with my eye the whole time on our present situation and the problems with which I was trying to deal. It is legitimate, indeed important, to use history in this way, but pure history I feel should be an

9

attempt to reconstruct the past without contemporary preoccupations. In particular I have not tried to write a history of religious thought. The concern of this book is with the impact of certain versions of Christianity on a secular tradition dealing with secular affairs. I am well aware that this must mean a concentration on the least important parts of religion, and I am also aware that what men think about their eternal destiny necessarily and profoundly affects their actions in temporal affairs, but it would be impossible to take all theology, or to take too much history for that matter, as coming within the terms of reference, and I have omitted much that is important in the purely religious history of the country, not denying its relevance but assuming it, and leaving it to others more expert in those matters than myself to handle.

Nor have I tried to discuss what ought to be the application of absolute Christian principles, ideally interpreted, to English society. My concern has not been with what ought to be, nor with what ought to have been, but with the results of what has been. The principles with which I have to deal have always been compromised by circumstances and always darkened by the particular limitations of the human mind peculiar to any period. In several cases, in the case for instance of the importance accorded to the peculiar rights of the individual man, or in that of the theory of the natural law, the origin is not apparently Christian, but these conceptions have been adopted by Christian thinkers, provided with Christian sanctions, made the vehicle of Christian values, and the important problem seems to be not whether these conceptions preceded Christianity, but whether they will survive it. Even when the ideas to be considered are Christian in origin they may well have been passed through a medium of social habit and common assumption which we would consider to be foreign to Christianity. For instance, most conceptions about the application of Christianity to social and political affairs before the nineteenth century seem to have assumed the inevitability of the division of society into sharply defined social classes with a mass of the under privileged and of the poor irredeemably at the bottom, an assumption which we of the twentieth century consider to be immoral and un-Christian. But we should be wrong to consider that the thought of those earlier Christians was morally valueless on that account, or that we can with sense disregard, or with safety abandon, all the tradition that comes to us with the marks of that thought upon it. Certainly such traditions must form a large part of the subject matter of my book.

Even to work within such limitations has taxed my historical knowledge to the full, indeed I have not included a bibliography since to have cited my authorities I would have had to put down a great deal of the mixed historical reading of about thirty years of adult life. Yet I would like to say that work on this subject suggests very strongly not that too much has been written on the matters that relate to it, but too little. It is strange how much English history has not been written, and how historians have tended to concentrate on certain subjects and to neglect others. Much excellent work has been done on the Puritans of the middle of the seventeenth century, but far too little on the Dissenters of the eighteenth, though there have been some very valuable contributions. Much has been done on the Wesleys and their immediate followers but far too little on the wider aspects of the great evangelical revival, its effects on a large variety of religious bodies, its relation to the romantic movement in literature, its importance in preparing for the nineteenth century, its course during that century. The problem of the relation of Church and state in England seems to have excited less interest among historians the nearer they got to the year 1900. The seventeenth century has been exhaustively treated, but admirable as has been the work upon their practical relationship in the eighteenth century there is still much more work to be done upon the theories of both eighteenth-century Churchmen and eighteenth-century Dissenters. Even more urgent is the need for a general historical work on Church and state covering the whole of the nineteenth century in England. However, very much of the religious history of the nineteenth century would repay the attention it might receive if only historians would resist the natural temptation to write more books on the early years of the Oxford Movement. Such work ought to be of great interest to the secular historian as well as to the ecclesiastical one. The nineteenth century was a very religious century, and if we are ever to attempt to understand nineteenth-century men and women and their doings we must consider carefully not only their religious controversies, but their great preachers, and their pious literature. Some day perhaps someone will realize how significant for the general social and intellectual history of England is the evidence that can be extracted from *Hymns*

Ancient and Modern, and the collections which preceded it. And the undisturbed dust on the bound volumes of printed sermons in most old libraries, or their lamentable appearance in the six-penny box on the second-hand book stalls, normally on the way to some more degrading fate, shows how lightly men have regarded a mass of important evidence on the accepted morality of the eighteenth and nineteenth centuries, the more important because so much of it is supremely commonplace, the work of mediocre men of reasonable ability and ordinary prejudices.

On some of these problems and on a little of this evidence I have ventured, though I am afraid but superficially and in such intervals as I could spare from very different work on very different subjects at Cambridge. I have however had some very valuable assistance. Canon Charles Smyth of Westminster read and commented on what has since become the first three chapters, then in an early form. Before I started writing I received from Dr. Helen Cam, Zemurray Professor at Harvard and Fellow of Girton College, certain very valuable suggestions for Chapter II, which she also read through and criticized in typescript. Chapters II and III were also subsequently and most helpfully criticized by Dr. W. Ullmann now of Cambridge. Professor Norman Sykes of Cambridge assisted me greatly by a rather drastic criticism of what has now become Chapters IV, V and VI, and Mr. F. Beckwith of the Leeds Library and Mr. F. R. Salter of Magdalene College, Cambridge, commented on Chapters VII and VIII, considering them at my request from the point of view of the Nonconformist. To all these I owe a very considerable debt, but I wish to make it plain that none of them have seen any part of the work in its final form and none of them have seen the whole work, nor have I accepted all their suggestions. I therefore alone must bear complete responsibility for everything in it. I also have to thank my publishers for their kindness and consideration throughout, and for their willingness to accept a book which through a stupid mistake of mine is about three times as long as the one they originally commissioned. Even so this book is unavoidably too short for so large a subject, but it is long enough if it suffices to lead men and women to consider and study this matter, while there is yet time.

I

THE PROBLEM

'Une nation est un principe spirituel résultant des complications profondes de l'histoire, une famille spirituelle non un group determiné par la configuration du sol.' E. Renan. Qu'est-ce qu'une nation?, Paris, 1882.

IT is unfortunate that the words 'The English Inheritance', and still more the words 'English Heritage', seem at first blush to suggest nothing so much as a very superior art calendar, the kind of calendar in which every month is illustrated by excellent photographs of such things as Ely Cathedral in the spring, a stretch of Sussex downs or Cornish coast in the summer and in the winter a half-timbered inn looking warm and hospitable in the snow; each page being adorned by a quotation from the less well-known lines of the better-known English poets. For the words have a romantic ring about them, and even if it is clear that the attempt to describe this heritage is going to be a little more serious in object and more continuous in style than can be the case with these excellent calendars it still might be supposed that what was intended would be illuminated by that attractive light which gilds armour and ruffle in old-fashioned historical novels. But all that is of course wrong. The words can have a perfectly realistic meaning. They mean whatever it is the English have inherited from their past; the English, it is to be noted, and not the British, for the words British must include the Scots and probably the Welsh and possibly the Irish, each of whom have a separate and valuable national inheritance of their own. And the English also were English before they were British. What has been inherited from their English past has been and still is of the greatest importance for themselves, for all the British and for the world. Much of it is lovely and of good report, some of it is ugly and pitiful, some of it perhaps sinister. Some of it would be best illustrated no doubt not by pictures of cathedrals in spring or downs in summer, but rather by the photographs of a derelict Dissenting chapel to whose grim walls spring seems to bring no new life, of a mean street where summer is only an infliction, or of a dingy public-house or gin palace where everything has been done to divorce conviviality from comfort. But good or bad, beautiful or ill favoured, it is all profoundly important and profoundly interesting, and all certainly worthy of description and systematic study in the most sober and realistic spirit of which man is capable.

Only of course to attempt to describe all that the English have inherited from their past without restriction would be to attempt the impossible. That is the next difficulty. They have clearly inherited from past centuries nearly all their institutions, a national position which they have recently defended but did not recently create, nearly all their literature, all their language, but a little slang, their social composition which they believe they are changing, their national habits and character which they believe to be unchanged, and most of their physical equipment. Even a generation which has fought so hard, suffered so much and apparently changed so much as the present must find that most of its environment and most of its possessions have been provided by the past, and the ways of thought and of practice inherited from its predecessors determine much more largely than it ever dreams how it will use the creations of the day or meet its needs. Clearly to describe all this in one short book would be impossible. Nor should it be necessary. There are already many excellent books specifically describing the English nation and the English spirit, and, further, it may be considered that every historian of English politics, English letters or life, indeed every historian of England or of some aspect of England has helped with the task.

There is indeed much that they could not describe. Usage, atmosphere, habit, style, all those distressingly illusive imponderables stand for much in national character, and they stand for much more in history than most historians can afford to confess. The ways that some men have dropped their H's or their G's, cocked their hats, arranged their rooms, drunk their liquor or talked through their noses have affected or symbolized the way that they thought, or that other men thought about them, to an extent that would make those things most important historical evidence, if only we could get exact records of them and could use it. These things were important, they are important; a very small amount of foreign travel, one meal at a French café, will soon suggest that in these things, often quite unconsciously inherited, are to be found some of the best clues to the mind of a nation, and some of the things that have helped to form it. But alas! these things evade the record; they hint at themselves in pictures, they suggest themselves in letters and contemporary novels and diaries, sometimes one can guess at their history, more often they are difficult to explain, often indeed too subtle even to describe, and when you try to gather them into a generalization you are still left only with an impression; and the work of many a talented writer has shown how dangerous it is to found historical analysis upon impressions alone. Sometimes a master of the historical craft can, with a phrase, a piece of description, a well-used adjective conjure them from the past. But that is often only for a transitory moment and normally they are wisely neglected and relegated to that larger and more important part of history which no man can ever write.

Now, I wish in this book neither to epitomize the work of all the historians who have described the heritage of England and how it was evolved, nor to try to describe the indescribable. I wish to essay a rather humbler task. Behind the conduct of English life, particularly behind the development of English institutions, as behind all life and all institutions, there are probably certain principles, certain values, respected if not always adequately observed or practised, which have partly controlled and directed men's actions, at least as far as the flesh and the devil would permit. In a country whose history has been so continuous as that of England, where men's minds have been so often controlled by traditional ways of thought slowly, almost unconsciously, adapted to the changing needs of modern practice, it is important to discover what these are, and I wish to discover and to discuss some of them. Of course it is to be realized that to separate a principle from the flesh and blood that entertains it is in some sort to falsify. History has indeed suffered much from the process of over-intellectualization. It has been written and taught too often as if men ever had been or could be controlled by motives and theories in the analysed desiccated state to which they are reduced for study. That is why it is necessary to remember at least the importance of atmosphere and the imponderables, and of practice as well as precept. But still, men are not wholly unintellectual, there is always some modicum of theory behind their actions even if it is unexpressed and almost entirely unrealized. What it is will be important, the more so if it is unrealized. And if the theoretical basis is abandoned it is possible that, though for a very long time all may seem to be the same on the surface, certain guides may be silent, certain restrictions no longer observed, and in due course there may be a change. Of course the change may be a change for the better; but perhaps the most important thing to recognize about a heritage is that it may be lost.

But even in this restricted sense there is not one English heritage, there are many. Within English life there are many historic divisions. There are local traditions, North and South, West Country and East Anglia, urban traditions, rural traditions, and the peculiar traditions of London or rather parts of London. Running across these are economic divisions, and social divisions often still regrettably strong, and groups with startlingly contrasted traditional values, as witness the conflict between the inherited standards of those who think that hunting, shooting and fishing are the proper occupations for a rightminded man, and those who think they are plainly the mark of the beast. Probably fewer people inherit their politics than they used to do, but party politics to some extent nowadays, and to a greater extent in the past, have helped to create different types of Englishmen with contrasted ways of thought. And behind these, often emphasizing the divisions of secular politics and giving them profundity, form and continuity, and passion, are the different religious traditions which have divided the country. Clearly what a man inherits from the past will differ according to whether he or his forebears are or were Roman Catholic, Church of England, Quaker, Wesleyan or Congregationalist or what-you-will. Indeed, probably the most persistent and penetrating permanent division in English history has been between Church of England man and Protestant Dissenter, causing a contrast in traditions which leaves its mark on the aesthetic, social and ethical preoccupations of many even of those who would be profoundly shocked to find that they had derived anything at all from any professedly Christian sect. Yet all are Englishmen, the very tension set up by their conflicts is an important part of the national heritage.

> Here the truceless armies yet
> Trample rolled in blood and sweat;
> They kill and kill and never die;
> And I think that each is I.

Perhaps that is an exaggeration. Sir Thomas More and Latimer, Campion and Barrow are dead long ago; in these matters we can perhaps afford to admire the heroism and let the hatreds go. The shots fired by Cavalier and Roundhead should awake now no echo in the hearts of living men; even the much more recently bitter feeling between Church and Dissent, or Conservative and Liberal, is largely forgotten, and modern party divisions fortunately do not seem to leave such permanently open wounds. Yet it would be untruthful not to record the fact that quarrels about essentials have formed a large part of the body of English history and misleading not to realize that in consequence what is derived from that history, consciously or unconsciously, will be different for different Englishmen.

But again I wish to restrict the enquiry. What I wish to do is to select certain points at which the Christian religion has intersected the history of the nation and helped to mould the national heritage. To do this without considering much that is secular would be unhistorical and wrong, but since this is my point of interest much secular history will necessarily be left out of the picture. Of course any selection must be partly individual and arbitrary, in fact it would be impossible to point to anything in the national tradition which has not been affected by a religion which most Englishmen have believed, or pretended to believe, for two thousand years. But I shall try to select certain points where the part that it has played seems to be important in the light of modern dilemmas. In my selection and in my treatment I may unwittingly show bias, and without intruding myself on my readers unduly I ought to declare my own position, that they may guess what my bias is likely to be. I am a member of the Church of England, neither High nor Low Church, but of the despised undistributed middle; I suppose I ought also to add that in secular politics I am a Conservative. I hope these things will not affect my enquiry, but if they do I can only ask my readers to pardon the frailty of the flesh and work things out for themselves. For if one thing can be said with assurance it is this: Christianity has affected profoundly our habits, our philosophy, our institutions, but with many of our people Christianity is becoming a fading memory, growing more dim and more misty as each year passes. In such case it is well to look forward to see what the result of its disappearance is likely to be, and to do this it is well to assess some of the things it has done in the past.

II

LAW AND FREEDOM

'561. The *Law of Nature* is that, which is Reason; which is Right and Fit. *Will* stands for nothing, in disjunction from Reason and Right: and our Apprehensions of Right are regulated by *the Nature of Things*. To give *Will* or *Power* for reason, is contrary to Reason. Will is no *Rule*, no *Justification* of any things.' BENJAMIN WHICHCOTE, D.D., *Moral and Religious Aphorisms*, ed. 1930, p. 65.

IN the old days the emphasis used to be on English freedom or liberty. To illustrate this it may be as well to take almost at random the expressions of two famous books of the past. 'Our Trimmer', wrote the Marquis of Halifax among the troubles of later Stuarts in his pamphlet on *The Character of a Trimmer*, 'Our Trimmer owneth a passion for liberty . . .; he taketh it hard for a Soul that doth not love Liberty ever to raise itself to another World; he taketh it to be the foundation of all virtue, and the only seasoning that giveth a relish to life.' The Trimmer was of course himself and the liberty he found in 'Our blessed Constitution, in which Dominion and Liberty are so well reconciled'.[1]

Or one may quote from Blackstone in his *Commentaries on the Laws of England*, written in the middle of the eighteenth century, which for a long time all students of law were supposed to read: 'The idea and practice of this political or civil liberty flourish in their highest vigour in these kingdoms, where it falls little short of perfection, and can only be lost or destroyed by the folly or demerits of its owner; the legislature, and of course the laws of England, being peculiarly adapted to the preservation of this inestimable blessing even in the meanest subject.'[2] The modern historian might have a word or two to say about the difference between the value of this liberty to the great noble of the seventeenth century or the academic lawyer of the eighteenth century

---

[1] *The Works of George Savile Marquess of Halifax*, edited with an Introduction by Walter Raleigh, Oxford 1912, pp. 61 and 62.

[2] Sir William Blackstone, Kt., *Commentaries on the Laws of England*, Sixteenth Edition, London 1825, Vol. I, p. 126 (Book I, Ch. I, 127).

and its value or reality to some of their half-brutalized contemporaries. Indeed so deeply impressed are we all about the slavery adverse economic conditions can impose, that phrases about 'this inestimable blessing' are perhaps a thought less fashionable than they were. However, the phrase, 'This is a free country, isn't it?' is a phrase one still hears from time to time in ordinary life. 'This is a free country, isn't it? And therefore I can . . .'— normally do something you very much dislike—keep fowls in my back garden, permit my daughter to practice her scales all morning, or express contempt at the bar of a public-house for the football of the Bolton Wanderers. Perhaps the phrase is normally reserved for the minor rubs of life, perhaps there may be a doubt nowadays about its applicability to more important matters; still, it has a good deal of history behind it, it expresses, vaguely, some sort of political philosophy, and its form is significant.

But probably nowadays in more official or considered utterances the emphasis would be laid not so much on the fact that England has been the home of freedom as the fact that she is a democracy. She is proud of her democratic constitution, she intends to make her social life more democratic, she leagues herself with other democratic powers, she accuses her enemies of planning an attack on democracy. Now no doubt something very important and valuable is expressed in these phrases. But it may be doubted if it ought to be considered as the whole of the English political heritage. After all it is only comparatively recently that 'democracy' has become a word of universal eulogy in the English language. Apparently this happened during the course of the nineteenth century. In the 'eighties, when Lord Randolph Churchill wished to adopt a name which would commend a popular form of Conservatism he called it Tory Democracy, but if you go back about forty years or a little more you will find, not Conservatives only, but others shaking their heads over democracy, as over something very questionable indeed. It was something French or American, and neither origin automatically commended it to all of our ancestors, who were normally men of prejudice. It meant the sweeping away of barriers, the levelling up of classes, the abolition of historic distinctions and other unpleasant processes which would end by leaving society at the mercy of the whirlwind of popular passion; and everyone knew from the story of the French Revolution what the result of that would be.

Of course the most natural rejoinder to that historical reflection is to remark how much that is valuable has been added in the last hundred years. And that is of course true. You have only to go and look at the holes and crannies where maids and footmen were supposed to sleep in a great house of the early years of the last century, or to imagine, for you are unlikely to be able to find them, the worst places where the poor then lived, to recognize that theirs was a world in which a little breaking down of barriers could have done no harm at all. Still, what our ancestors said was not wholly absurd and is not wholly irrelevant. For as most people know there is rather a serious ethical problem which may be raised by the working of democracy. It is probably so well understood that it may seem not to be right to waste time and space upon it, but since it is rather important for the argument of this chapter it is worth while at least to draw attention to it as shortly as possible.

It lies partly but not wholly in the problem of minorities. The justification of the force and if need be of the severity of the law in a democracy is that it is the will of all and made for the good of all. That is the theory. Of course in many cases the law may be at best the will of a majority and the rather bewildered indirectly expressed will of the majority at that; and it may be at best only made for the good of the majority. That may of course be still perfectly justifiable, no one could presumably wish that the minor interests of a section of the people should impede what is necessary for the welfare of the whole. What a minority has got to do in such circumstances is to persuade enough people that its interests are not an impediment to the welfare of the whole, in fact to gain the protection of the majority, and if they cannot do that they must bear their misfortune. But supposing what is at stake is not just the interests of a minority, but the very existence of a large minority, or at least all that makes life tolerable or desirable for it? And supposing there is not and so far as can be seen never will be any chance of making the majority relent? In such a situation a serious ethical problem may be involved. Such situations may be difficult to envisage in a more or less homogeneous community like Great Britain, but they are even probable in what are called plural communities, normal enough in Asia, where one race or religion lives permanently with another in a permanent and sharply defined minority. Indeed, such situations have presented the most obstinate difficulties in the task of extending self-government in the British Empire. Nor are such communities confined to Asia; they are to be found in Eastern Europe, and even in the rest of Europe it has been demonstrated that a comparable situation may exist and make life intolerable for the Jews where there is strong anti-Semitism among the majority of the people.

Besides this, if democracy is simply defined as government in which the will of the people prevails it is important to know how that will has been formed. Otherwise there is no guarantee at all that that will may not have been called into existence by cruel and ruthless men using all the devices with which modern technique has equipped the state, the wireless, the control of publicity, the control of education, till that will is turned to ends as wicked and as dreadful as themselves; and modern experience shows very clearly what may happen then.

Therefore though democracy, true democracy, that is, with free public opinion and really free elections, may be a necessary part of the constitution of a modern state, the best safeguard for the retention and development of those things which humanity holds valuable, and may hold out the best hopes for the development of that social justice which our forefathers so noticeably failed to secure, yet even at its best the ideal is not ethically comprehensive enough to stand alone. You cannot be content simply to say that the will of the people must prevail, you must add to that the rider that it must be the will of the people, who must realize that there are certain things the people ought not to do, even when a majority of the people wishes very much to do them; it must be the will of the people expressed in a certain way, engendered in certain conditions which must allow the free expression of opinions, even of opinions which may seem absurd and repugnant to the ordinary man. In fact the will of the people may be allowed to prevail with safety only if the people realize that they are not the final and sovereign power in the universe.

These things may be truisms. After thirty years' experience of 'people's courts' and of concentration and labour camps for 'the enemies of the people' it would need a very bold man to say that they are truisms that do not need to be repeated. But it may be said that at least these things do not need to be repeated in relation to England. It would be as well not to be too sure of that; but if there is any truth in that statement at all, it is true because with the theory of democracy something else has been retained from an older world, something which assisted democracy to develop, which may need democracy to complete it, but whose place democracy can by itself never completely with safety supply.

But to discover this thing we must return to our old predemocratic writers. What they were talking about was freedom protected by law. 'Our Trimmer', so Halifax starts his pamphlet, 'as he hath a great Veneration for laws in general, so he hath a more particular for our own, he looketh upon them as the Chains that tie up our unruly Passions, which else, like wild Beasts let loose, would reduce the world into its first State of Barbarism and Hostility; the good things we enjoy we owe to them; and the ill things we are freed from is by their Protection.'[1] It is 'of course the laws of England' which with the legislature are for Blackstone 'peculiarly adapted' to preserve for everyman the inestimable blessing of civil liberty, even for the meanest subject. The conception was that a man should be able to live his life under the protection of a law which would prevent him being wantonly and arbitrarily interfered with to suit the whim, passing need, or momentary passion of another human being, be he private person or official. If a man were to be beggared or imprisoned or hanged, or even compelled to do something he did not wish to do or forbidden to do something which he wished, it should at least be according to a known rule, settled beforehand, not created or modified to meet his case and administered by a court that would take such a rule as its guide and not the commands of authority; and if others tried to interfere with him he could invoke such rule to prevent them. In fact he should be under the rule of law and not in what in the sixteenth century was reputed to be the condition of the Turks, 'Among whom there is no right, law nor commonwealth contract, but only the will of the Lorde and segnior'.[2]

The opposite to the 'rule of law' is often called 'arbitrary power'. But there is a difficulty here. If arbitrary power is equated with discretionary power, that is a power which grants to men in authority some measure of freedom to make up their own minds on the facts before them and to deal within prescribed limits with their subjects accordingly, then no state, no judiciary, no not even a borough police authority could do its work

[1] Halifax, op. cit., p. 50.
[2] Smith, De Republica Anglorum, ed. L. Alston, Cambridge 1906, p. 21.

properly without arbitrary power. Such power will be needed to meet emergencies, it will be needed to secure equity, since any predetermined rule blindly and rigidly applied to all cases may well cause injustice and folly, it is probably needed to secure ordinary efficient government. Yet the discretion of authorities is apt to interfere with what seem to private people to be their rights, and if the discretion is too wide and vague it is clear that the rule of law may be of no avail.

It is a problem which has caused some of the great dilemmas of English history. In Stuart times, and indeed before, the king by right of his kingly office and to serve the needs of his kingdom claimed a discretion so wide and so inadequately restricted by the courts that many even of his most sober subjects came to believe that their rights were not secure. In the present century, in order to meet the complicating fluctuating needs of modern society, parliament has developed the habit of surrendering to ministers and others powers so wide and so numerous that men have felt that their lives lie at the mercy of government regulations. But into these interesting dilemmas we need not penetrate. In the last resort it is principle that matters. As the seventeenth century suggests, if the right principle is firmly grasped the dilemmas of its application can, after controversy, be resolved. In principle there is all the difference in the world between the discretion of a government which recognizes that its subjects have clearly established rights which it is its duty to respect, indeed that the object of its discretion is in the last resort the defence of those rights, and the power of a government whose subjects are simply at disposal to be used for its own purposes as government thinks fit. And the English have felt, one might almost say throughout their history, that between themselves and the 'Turk-like' condition has stood their conception of the rule of law.

In fact the rule of law in some form is probably a necessary pre-condition for any form of civilized life or any form of freedom. Unless a man can know where he is, unless some area of his life and activity is reasonably protected from habitual interference by others at their will, he cannot be called free without a grave abuse of language. But even so by itself the rule of law is not enough, it suffers from two defects. The rule of law is no protection against the law-makers. It can possibly restrain an official (if the law has not given him discretion), it cannot possibly restrain a sovereign parliament; and a legislature can act as arbitrarily as an individual. The obvious example of this has always been an act of attainder, that is, an act of parliament directed against an individual, reciting in the preamble certain offences of which he is alleged to be guilty, though he may not have been tried, and decreeing a penalty against him in the body of the act. But it would be easy to find more modern examples in more up-to-date technique.

The other defect of the rule of law is that the laws may be bad, and so they were in England at least before about 1824: in many ways very bad. Blackstone himself rather later in his work confesses in a famous passage that 'It is a melancholy truth, that among the variety of actions which men are daily liable to commit, no less than an hundred and sixty have been declared by act of parliament to be felonies without benefit of clergy; or, in other words, to be worthy of instant death'.[1] And he goes on to stigmatize the results of this system. 'Melancholy' is indeed a mild word for that dreadful list of actions, some trivial offences, some hardly offences at all, for which our forefathers had prescribed the gallows. It is true that in many cases the sentence was commuted, but that fact itself introduced an uncertainty and lack of equality into the operation of the law which was intolerable, and outrageous severity was always possible.[2] Nor was the frequency of the sentence of death the only defect of the old English legal system; and if one is inclined to praise the English law as the defence of the individual against the government it is worthwhile to turn to the state trials and read one or two of the sixteenth- or seventeenth-century trials for treason. The accused is not defended by counsel, the law has been construed at many points to his disadvantage, he cannot compel his witnesses to attend, he has probably lain in prison for some time. In the sixteenth or very early seventeenth century he or his accomplices may have been tortured, and he is pressed by the best legal intelligence of his day, acting with savage gusto, along a *via dolorosa* which leads almost inevitably to the terrible sentence of degrading and painful death, with probable beggary for all his dependants.

It is perhaps wrong to judge these things by modern standards with minds sharpened by modern sensitiveness to suffering. Even in eighteenth-century England values were different from ours and life was cheaper, while before and indeed after 1600 the

---

[1] Blackstone, *op. cit.*, Vol. IV, p. 18 (Book IV, Ch. I, 19).
[2] See L. Radzinowicz, *A History of Criminal Law*, London 1948, Vol. I *passim*.

domestic order of the state, which traitors jeopardized, was viewed with a fierce anxiety that is not easily understood by a generation that can look back on two hundred years of internal peace disturbed by nothing more serious than riots. But even if one tries to strip away from oneself modern susceptibilities luxuriantly developed in the hot-house of modern domestic security, even if one tries to live again in a harsher more dangerous world and to concede, moreover, a sanctity to the rights of property which no modern man could concede, yet even so the vagaries of the English criminal law as well as its wayward thirst for blood still seem to prove that the principle of the rule of law is not by itself enough to secure for men the treatment they have a right to demand.

Yet even if English history demonstrates the defects of the rule of law, it also demonstrates its value. Bad as it may have been, the tough old English law was good enough at least for one purpose, and that a most important one. It prevented England from becoming an absolute monarchy on the model of Louis XIV. In the rugged, unpleasing personality of a great seventeenth-century lawyer, Chief Justice Coke, it confronted the person of James I and at a critical moment prescribed limits to the prerogative of the crown. In the struggle between king and parliament which developed then, parliament relied on the law; it gave form and force to its case. As the struggle developed it is true both sides violated the law; neither side found in it a satisfactory answer to their need for a political philosophy, but each fell back upon it as a citadel in time of need; and in the end the revolution of 1688 which completed the crisis was in result and object, as Macaulay said, 'a preserving revolution', its aim was to preserve the law, as parliament conceived it, so that it might restrain governments and preserve freedom. Indeed it is not too much to say that at a critical period in human development the English law with all its defects performed a function for human freedom which no other power in the world could have performed.

And it is only fair to remember that with all its defects in its long history it produced institutions and methods which have been of great avail in the prevention of injustice and persecution. In the course of English legal history there emerged trial by jury, the independence of judge and jury, the principle of habeas corpus by which any man suffering imprisonment can put the law into motion, and in time the principle of equality before the law, though that last principle at least is not one which English medieval feudal lawyers could have accepted. These things are perhaps not honoured to-day as they used to be. Men have occupied themselves in pointing out how economic inequality may nullify the benefit of them all, or how there have always been exceptions to their usefulness, or even in creating exceptions to their operation to meet urgent modern needs. Yet you only have to study the workings of justice in countries where neither these things, nor any substitute for them, have been sincerely tried to realize how inestimably valuable they are.

The victory of the law was possible only because England was a country whose soil was impregnated with law. Law complicated and hazardous brooded over the country house, so that it was desirable for its owner either to know something of its intricacies or to have access to someone who did if he was to maintain his position. It was supposed to control his proceedings when he entered the justice room to give rule and discipline to his poorer neighbours, and it could provide sharp discipline for himself if it came to the notice of the higher courts that he had overridden it. It brooded over the village, exacting public duties from selected villagers, perhaps as parish constables or overseers of the poor, or even those whose duty it was to mend the roads. It lay in wait for everyman, and was that by which the position or property of everyman was supposed to be safeguarded. For a period many even of those who were not going to practise were educated at the Inns of Court. In Shakespeare's *Henry IV, Part II*, Mr. Justice Shallow claimed to have been educated at Clement's Inn where he thought that they remembered 'Mad Shallow yet'. Sir John Falstaff was of opinion that Shallow exaggerated the boldness of his disorders, a point on which Sir John was something of an authority, yet he had probably been no very valuable student. If so, others were more assiduous. Maitland in his *English Law and the Renaissance* points out that young men at the Inns of Court in the mid-sixteenth century wrangled in mock legal contest using the execrable Latin and French which were their terms of art with a vigour that surprised that cultivated Elizabethan Sir Thomas Smith, but which, as Maitland points out, shows the virility of the system.[1]

Law penetrated all things, it entered into language, into thought, into Shakespeare's plays to such an extent that that

[1] F. W. Maitland, *English Law and the Renaissance*, Cambridge 1901.

has been part of the case that they were actually written by a great lawyer, and always into politics. Lawyers penetrated everywhere. They filled the government service, they advised the opponents of government, where such were bold enough to exist, they filled the House of Commons. Of course the crowding of the public service with lawyers was not peculiar to England, but in England they were mostly men trained in the native English law and not in the Roman law so popular on the Continent, a more elegant code perhaps, but also a better friend to absolute monarchies. Small wonder that the Tudors were to accept the ancient law of England as a sturdy if barbarous ally. Small wonder that when the Stuarts stumbled against what most contemporary Englishmen imagined the law to be they were brought down into the dust.

This drenching of English life and consciousness with the sense of law, with the rights of law, with the methods of law, with the obligations of law, was very old, even if sixteenth- and seventeenth-century lawyers mistook the nature of that antiquity. Law formed much of the framework of later medieval society; even in the troubled fifteenth century the nobility and gentry had varied their pastime of cutting each other's throats with much tortuous litigation. Law had been the resource of many who had opposed the crown, and at an earlier stage had been the medium by which strong medieval kings had imposed their duties upon all men. But it went further back still, back beyond the Norman Conquest, when William I expressed his desire that his subjects should have and hold the laws of King Edward the Confessor with the additions he had made to them, back into periods where scholars move with the greatest caution, for all is controversial. Probably it went right back to a pre-Christian world in which for the free man there was an elaborate code of personal rights and personal obligations and a strong sense of justice, perhaps such as can be studied in the Icelandic sagas, which indeed depict a society kindred to that from which some of our ancestors are sprung.

Many of the experiences, many of the ideas to which England was subjected were shared by other nations in Western Europe, but the proportions of the mixture and the component parts are never quite the same in one nation as in another, and the fortunes of history are different; that is indeed why there are such things as nations. England is an island, since the eleventh century not

easy to conquer, but possibly easy to unite, while probably even before that time something in the Saxon and Scandinavian basic elements had already given a distinctive flavour. Certainly England has been profoundly affected for all time by the fact that she was at certain periods one of the best organized of medieval kingdoms, no doubt owing much in this matter to the genius of such a man as Henry II. Still more important is the fact that her history has been unusually continuous, often diversified by violence and catastrophe, but with the old never wholly erased by the new; in fact always a more or less successful attempt to mix the old wine with the new and patch the old bottles.

Therefore is it fanciful to believe that the nature of this prolonged legal apprenticeship can explain something of the English character? As there was no moment at which a new coherent set of ideas was substituted for the old as in France by the Revolution, so there was no moment at which, in modern times at least, a scientific code was received from the hands of a single lawmaker. Therefore Englishmen have been apt to look for guidance neither to abstract principle nor to government officials, but backwards to long experience of living in a community which was a complex of individual rights and personal obligations, which they had to vindicate for themselves or to perform for themselves, and a community in which they have had much varied experience of self-government. Much of English law was of course in fact derived from above, from royal decree, or parliamentary legislation, if some also came from local custom. But it remained in action so long, was so richly glossed by precedent, became so mixed with habits of the people that it came to seem to be the product of life rather than of legislation, to be the rule, that is, which the experience and the consciences of men had imposed as the proper method of living together in a body politic.

With so much continuous corporate life to look back upon it has perhaps been natural that the appeal has been to practice rather than to theory, and it has not been for nothing that freedom has been said in England to 'broaden down from precedent to precedent', and not from principle to principle. This may have meant that the Englishman's sense of justice in the abstract has not been strong, and that he has failed to recognize the value of theory, a failure which is often the penalty of successful practice. But has it not meant in compensation that he has had an ingrained sense of order and justice based not on the words of philosophers or on the acts of statesmen, but on the habits developed by living together for centuries in a society ordered by custom and based firmly on the personal obligations of its members and instructed in the art of practical compromise by long political experiences? Does not this habit appear in the wonderfully orderly behaviour of the queues which English men and women form outside shops, in the games that they play, in the sometimes almost laboriously orderly conduct of their clubs and societies? In all these matters Englishmen submit freely to codes of conduct self-devised and completely voluntary, and they are matters in which the state cannot enter at all.

This may be fanciful, but there is one important fact about the ancient, partly traditional, character of that law which is better established and which raises a point of the most urgent, the most modern importance. I said that there were two defects which might negative the usefulness of the rule of law standing by itself, first that the rule of law was no defence against the law-makers, and second that the law which ruled might in itself be bad. The second defect can be removed by reform, the first can never be removed. In our modern conception law must be the command of a law-making body and, ultimately, either directly or by delegation, of what is called a sovereign law-making body. Even if the actual law is based on custom, or created by the precedent laid down by a judge in a particular court, it exists as it is only by the permission of some law-making body which could change it, or negative it, should that seem good. For according to the theories of most jurists there must be in every state, in domestic matters, a power called the sovereign power which can make any law, change any law or repeal any law, and against which there can be no appeal; and these theories would seem to be based on an accurate view of the necessities of the case. History does certainly seem to suggest that a growing or changing community cannot accept the permanent control of any body of custom or law which it cannot also change to fit the needs of the time. Nor can such a community permit its order to be permanently imperilled, or the wishes and safety of the majority to be recklessly flouted, by an appeal to ancient custom or right, or to the vagaries of the individual conscience. Thus even when a constitution guarantees particular laws and places them beyond the power of the ordinary parliament or assembly, there is normally nowadays

C

provision for change somewhere in the constitution. But if such sovereign power, at least in domestic matters, is probably necessary, it is also certainly dangerous. The laws can be so made, or so modified, that the rule of law becomes simply systematized injustice. The Nuremberg decrees made by the Nazis against the Jews, if they were consistently administered, might be considered after a sort to be the rule of law, but they were none the less a crime against humanity.

Now in the world of the Middle Ages this sovereign law making power in any community was not an idea which the ordinary man could at all easily entertain. For one thing any state in Western Christendom was part and parcel of a Church which claimed to be universal, and that meant there was a whole area of human life for which the local king and parliament could no more legislate than they could for the subjects of the Cham of Tartary. The extent of that area was doubtful, there were constant squabbles about its boundaries, but its existence at all was a standing obstacle to the conception of sovereignty. The point was put clearly by Sir Thomas More on his way to martyrdom for refusing to accept King Henry VIII as supreme head of the Church, when he was asked at his trial to give reason why sentence of death should not be passed on him. To quote Ropers' Life, ' "For as much as, my Lord," quoth he, "this Indictment is grounded uppon an acte of parliamente directly repugnant to the lawes of God and his holye Churche the supreeme government of which or of any part whereof may no temporal prince presume by any lawe to take uppon him as rightfully belonging to the Sea of Roome. . . . It is therefore in lawe amongst Christen men insufficient to charge any Christen man." '[1] The act was not only bad, it was not law, although passed by parliament.

But it was not only in religious matters that there might be limitations in men's minds on any law making or law changing power. Much of the law was held to be derived from custom, to be informed by ancient wisdom, to come from ancient and irrevocable royal grant. By these things men held their rights and who should take them from them? Indeed surely they held these things by the same law as the king held his throne, and if he broke that he ceased to be a lawful king and became a tyrant, and then— but there was considerable controversy about what should happen

[1] William Roper, *The Lyfe of Sir Thomas Moore, knighte,* edited by E. V. Hitchcock, E.E.T.S., Orig. Series No. 197, p. 92.

then. And if there were things the king could not do, what about parliament? Even into the seventeenth century there lingered some idea that it was perhaps right for the judges to put aside acts of parliament as unlawful. As Chief Justice Coke said: 'In many cases the common law will control acts of Parliament, and sometimes adjudge them to be utterly void.'[1]

Chief Justice Coke was not however a systematic thinker and there is some controversy about what his view about the relation of the judges to parliament actually was, or whether it was consistent over the whole of his career. Certainly the fact of parliamentary sovereignty was proved to be a necessity in the seventeenth century. The law was not adequate to the task of settling the relations of king and parliament, it was too obscure and doubtful, and in actual fact, though many men disguised this from themselves and their neighbours by much misused learning, if rightly administered it gave too much power to the king. Therefore the law had to be changed by parliament exerting pressure on the king to gain his assent. Certainly it would not have been tolerable to allow judges, appointed by the king, to declare any parliamentary statute to be 'utterly void', indeed it was found to be necessary in the end to take from the king that power of dispensing with statutes in certain individual cases which he had always possessed. Indeed the results of the seventeenth century left a position in which a parliamentary statute which had received the assent of king, lords, and commons was something which in law could override everything, but which nothing could override.

But this fact has much less importance for our purposes than would at first sight appear, and to understand why this is, it is better to turn back to Blackstone, writing well over one hundred years after Coke had died and after parliament had achieved its supremacy. Blackstone recognized there must be in all forms of government 'A supreme, irresistible, absolute, uncontrolled authority, in which the *jura summa imperii*, or the rights of sovereignty reside', and 'by the sovereign power', he says clearly, 'is meant the making of laws'.[2] He found that power in king and

---

[1] C. H. McIlwain, *The High Court of Parliament and Its Supremacy*, Yale University Press 1910, p. 286. (But see whole chapter on Relations of Judiciary and Legislature.) Cf. W. S. Holdsworth, K.C., D.C.K., *A History of English Law*, Vols. IV, V, 1924, Vol. V, pp. 478–85, Vol. VI, pp. 82–6.

[2] Blackstone, *op. cit.*, Vol. I, p. 48 (Introduction, s2, 49).

parliament working in conjunction.[1] Nevertheless he cannot have conceived parliament as being perfectly free to do what it liked, there were certain things which it had not created and could not abrogate; for elsewhere he says: 'Those rights then which God and nature have established, and which are therefore called natural rights, such as are life and liberty need not the aid of human laws to be more effectually invested in every man than they are; neither do they receive any additional strength when declared by the Municipal laws to be inviolable, on the contrary, no human legislature has power to abridge or destroy them, unless the owner shall himself commit some act that amounts to a forfeiture. . . . For that legislature in all these cases acts only . . . in subordination to the great lawgiver, transcribing and publishing his precepts.'[2]

At first sight to talk about the existence of a supreme authority in every state on one page and on another to say that there were certain things which no legislature has power to do seems to be indulging in something like a contradiction in terms. Of course you could resolve the paradox by saying that the one statement applies to legal power and the other to moral right, though the form of his statement about the power of a human legislature does not seem completely to bear this out. But that the conflict might not seem so important to Blackstone as it is urgent for us may I think be revealed by his description of what should be the objects of the statutes passed by this supreme parliament. 'Statutes also', he says, 'are either declaratory of the Common Law, or remedial of some defects therein.' Possibly it may be necessary to declare anew old customs that had fallen into disuse or even become disputable or 'to supply such defects, or abridge such superfluities in the Common Law, as arise either from the general imperfections of all human laws, from change of time and circumstance, from the mistakes and inadvised determinations of unlearned (or even learned) judges, or from any cause whatsoever'.[3] Parliament was to improve, to regulate, to supply what the times might make necessary, but it was not to create. The system was already there. It was not the task of parliament to work out an entirely new scheme of relationships between man and man, those relationships had been already established,

---

[1] Blackstone, *op. cit.*, Vol. I, p. 50 (Introduction, s2, 51).
[2] *Ibid.*, p. 85 (Introduction, s2, 87).
[3] *Ibid.*, p. 53 (Introduction, s3, 54).

established once and for all by the Creator of the universe, established for England by the traditional wisdom of the law. It was a view of its functions which a parliament of landowners and lawyers was likely to share, and even if one house for a moment forgot itself it must be remembered that in Blackstone's view each house of parliament had a separate entity in a balanced constitution with each house balanced against the other and both balanced against the king, so that any part of the constitution might be checked by the others from acting unadvisedly. Both Coke and Blackstone were anxious about the harm which might be done to the law by members of either house of parliament who were ignorant of it and tried to mend it, or who in deciding matters before them, in Coke's words, forsook the 'golden metwand' of the law for the 'crooked cord of discretion', but both could safely assume that the general object of parliament was to preserve the law, not to destroy it.[1]

If you grant this assumption, the sovereignty of king in parliament is a very innocuous doctrine indeed, and is not in the least likely to conflict with the theoretical restrictions which Blackstone presupposes for all law-making bodies. But the form in which he expresses those restrictions is important. Remember he talks about 'those rights which God and nature have established', 'such as are life and liberty'. And Halifax, our other witness, also speaks of the law of nature. 'God himself', he says, 'thought it not enough to be a Creator, without being a lawgiver, and His goodness had been defective towards mankind in making them, if He had not prescribed rules to make them happy too. All laws flow from that of nature, and where that is not the Foundation they may be legally imposed, but they will be lamely obeyed.'[2] That is, in the conception of both, behind the activities of the human legislator, there was conceived to be a system of rules which it was his duty to observe, rules which sprang from the nature of an ordered universe and in the last resort from the will of Almighty God who had created and ordered that universe.

Now the idea that there was something in society which the ruler or king could not rightly set aside was very ancient. As I

[1] For a very interesting discussion on the old conception of the nature of law see Burke's *Tracts on the Popery Laws*, Ch. III, Part I. *The Works of the Right Hon. Edmund Burke,* ed. 1812, Vol. IX, pp. 344 ff.

[2] Halifax, *op. cit.*, p. 50.

have said the idea of justice which entails the recognition of the rights of the individual is probably pre-Christian. I have suggested that you may find it in the Icelandic sagas, but to go back to a very different portion of antiquity, if Ahab had been absolute sovereign of Israel he could have expropriated Naboth, that obvious *kulak*, and taken his vineyard, and there would have been no need for Jezebel to fake an accusation of treason. But Naboth's right to the vineyard was acknowledged; fraud and injustice was needed to deprive him of it. Yet even if the idea of justice was pre-Christian, it was one the Christian Church took in her stride. She took it upon herself to rebuke unjust kings, as Elijah had rebuked Ahab. At the coronation she consecrated the king to his holy task of maintaining justice, and at that service the king had to swear that he would observe the law. It was an oath which might be said to lie at the centre of medieval society, and from the later middle ages he swore to obey the law which his people had chosen, or perhaps the right form was even 'should chose'. In theory the medieval king might have very great powers, such powers as might be necessary to enable him to perform the difficult task of government, but his subjects had rights too, rights which he must in no way take from them unless he was to cease to be a lawful king and become a tyrant like Ahab.

Those rights, unless they forfeited them, included the possession of their property, of their lives and limbs, and some freedom of choice, as the later form of the coronation oath shows. For if men have an inherent right to their position in the world then they have a right to share in decisions which may affect that position, what touches all should be approved by all, and the force of law comes from the assent of all. As Richard Hooker, with whom in a moment we shall have dealings, wrote at the close of the sixteenth century: 'Laws they are not therefore, which public approbation hath not made so.' The authority of the high court of parliament sprang not only from the fact that it was the highest court of law in the land, not only from the fact that the king's throne was set up in the midst of it and that it therefore spoke with his dread authority, but also from the fact that every man was conceived to be present there, either in person or by attorney, so that his assent could be given to what was done.

In all this I have grossly over-simplified very complicated

things and dealt, I am afraid, dogmatically with very controversial matters. Obviously, even if I had the knowledge, I could not sum up the thought and feeling of many centuries in a few short paragraphs. Moreover the matter always bristled with unresolved problems. There was the king's power, which was certainly necessary, and probably of divine origin, to be fitted in. The needs of public peace and public safety were always urgent. It was freely acknowledged that it was necessary to make particular laws to fit the particular needs of various communities, as such needs became apparent.[1] But what I have tried to emphasize is the prevalence of the feeling emerging from primitive times, but consecrated by Christianity, that behind the activities of earthly rulers and law-makers there was a body of rights, which they had not created and could not take away without forfeiting their own claims to their own position.

Now this is expressed by Blackstone not in the ancient form of special rights and privileges and properties which might be the special birthright of individuals, but in the generalized philosophical and universal form of the law of nature under which men and women had their rights and duties as men and women by a law which was common to all reasonable creatures.

Here too the origins are pre-Christian. The conception of a law of nature has a long and distinguished ancestry in the pagan classical world, it is indeed one of the most valuable moral legacies which that world left behind it. Perhaps it may even be post-Christian also. Just as the idea of a common code which all humanity shared, or ought to share, could be conceived by pagan lawyers and philosophers who had not yet received the Christian revelation of the nature of God, so perhaps it may still be maintained by those who have rejected any belief in that revelation or in any system of transcendent values which the nature of the universe prescribes. Where it cannot be based on the will of a God or on the laws of an ordered universe it must be based on the needs and convenience of man, and in a world which beyond all former ages rejects universal moral sanctions one may hope sincerely such foundations may be a secure basis for human rights. One must hope, but one may doubt. What cannot rest on the will of God must rest on the will of man, and to assume that our

[1] See Helen Cam, Litt.D., *The Legislators of Medieval England*, the Raleigh Lecture on History for the British Academy, 1945, *Proceedings of the British Academy*, Vol. XXXI.

view of man's needs and rights will always and everywhere affect men's actions and opinions is to credit to our ideas a universality and a permanence which neither history nor probability encourages us to assume. Indeed it is significant that our conception of natural law and natural laws has largely come to us from men who whatever their philosophy were not modern materialists or agnostics, and it has largely come to us interpreted by Christians who saw it as the code of a world for which God had decreed laws which men have the intelligence to apprehend, and should use their free will to observe.

For the conception of a law of nature was one of which in various forms many Christian lawyers and philosophers made great use. To Christians it presented the problem of the relations of the universal law revealed to man by the secular reason which God has granted to all men, with the laws of universal validity which He has revealed by the incarnation, through the Church and in the Scriptures. That question has been systematically answered by one of the greatest of all Christian philosophers, St. Thomas Aquinas, whose whole treatment of the idea of natural law has had a very wide influence on all Western European civilization. However, in dealing with the specifically English inheritance it is convenient to turn to an Englishman, and to an Englishman who was for some time widely read in his own country.

Richard Hooker, as the sixteenth century closed and the seventeenth century opened, wrote what came to be a standard apology for the Church of England, his *Laws of the Ecclesiastical Polity*, and in the first book he described his conception of the law, or rather of the various laws, of the universe. For him the law of nature is that of the physical universe, the law by which the stars move and the grass grows, the law of reason is that system which God has given man reason to apprehend as the things which belong to his peace, the law of revelation comes from what He had revealed of Himself and His purpose in Holy Scripture, and all are emanations of what is far above man's comprehension the Law of the Being of God Himself. 'Wherefore,' he says, 'that here we may briefly end: of Law there can be no less acknowledged than that her seat is the bosom of God, her voice the harmony of the world: all things in heaven and earth do her homage, the very least as feeling her care, and the greatest as not exempted from her power: both Angels and men and creatures of what condition soever, though each in different sort and manner, yet all with uniform consent, admiring her as the mother of their peace and joy.'[1]

It is a lofty conception, and yet men could dare to think that the old pedantic, crabbed, unreasonable, gallows-shadowed English law was in some way related to it; and when one considers the services of that law to freedom, if freedom is part of the law of the universe, if it is the condition that God has willed for His children, their thought may not have been entirely without reason. Be that as it may, here surely is a point at which Christianity intersects our national history. It consecrates the idea of justice which gives its ultimate authority to the rule of law and it gives its authority to the conception of the law of nature, which gives philosophical endorsement to that idea.

But what has all this to do with us now? It may be a pleasing phantasy to see the idea of justice present in the habits and the instincts of the English, their actual legal and constitutional arrangements can have no place any longer for the ideal for a fundamental unalterable law. Nor for that matter are we likely to have any further use for those ideas. History may traverse parallel paths but it never crosses precisely the same ground. We are not likely to face the dangers of Stuart rule in our day, and if we have to confront the much worse tyranny of the modern totalitarian state we will not be able to protect ourselves with black letter authorities or legal precedents, or an appeal to justice either natural or divine; habeas corpus would simply not come into the picture when the Gestapo or the N.K.V.D. knocked at our door in the middle of the night. Even were our own government inclined to authoritarian methods we may be quite sure that it would equip itself for the purpose with powers which were legally unassailable by using the legislative powers of parliament, against which the appeal to positive law would be no protection at all. Nor is our conception of the order of nature the same as that which impressed men so deeply in medieval times or in the sixteenth or seventeenth centuries, and the words 'nature' or 'natural' have proved themselves to be so extremely equivocal, and to be capable of meaning so many different things, as to be very uncertain allies in the work of definition. We live certainly in a period dominated by sovereign states which are at the least

[1] Richard Hooker, *Of the Laws of Ecclesiastical Polity*. Ed. 1865, Vol. I, Book I, XVI, 8, p. 228.

complete masters in their own houses; if haply we may live towards the end of that period.

Moreover there is one further point to be borne in mind. The idea of a law which cannot be changed naturally tends to be in some sort a conservative idea. It may claim its validity from the fact that it pretends to safeguard the rights of all individuals, it has gained its force in the past from the fact that it did safeguard the properties and privileges of those who were articulate enough and powerful enough to make their views felt. Now we are all of us impressed by the need to set right the injustices and the lack of freedom which arise from the economic inequalities of society. It is therefore important to consider the possibility that the conception of an unchangeable law, unless carefully handled, might seem to be, might even become an impediment to necessary progress.

Yet in spite of all these considerations it seems to me that these old ideas may have something of value to suggest in our endeavour to find some answer to our modern problems. For we have to face serious modern problems. Democracy is not an idea which can safely stand by itself, unless it is recognized that there are some things the people may not do. The rule of law is not ethically complete unless it is clear that the law is something else than the arbitrary policy of the legislator. Even the struggle for social and economic justice can be made the excuse for awful crimes against millions of people unless there is something to restrict what is done in its name. Indeed so much is intrinsically likely, for statesmen tend to take the best ideals of an age as cover for their worst actions. In the sixteenth and seventeenth centuries they took cover behind religion, in the twentieth Hitler called the forces he controlled 'National Socialism'. Therefore the idea of economic equality needs also something to complete it, if it is to be made safe for humanity.

What then is the missing piece of the jigsaw puzzle? Many people believe that their security lies in the common sense and common humanity of ordinary people. I do not want to be put in a concentration camp, you do not want to be put into a concentration camp, neither of us wishes to see anyone else put into a concentration camp, therefore no one will ever put anyone into a concentration camp ever again. No doubt here is a force to be reckoned with, for which we can thank God, but it is a force whose strength most people wildly exaggerate. The history of two wars has proved that circumstances may change people's feelings in this matter more than they could ever dream to be possible, if the matter only rests upon common feeling. If the matter rests only on a common sense of expediency, it is well to remember that history suggests that it is impossible to forecast in what direction, and to what lengths, expediency as a guide, acting on its own, may lead; and it is likely that humanity will be led not by your sense of expediency, nor by mine, but by someone else's, the sense of someone who is by temper forceful enough to achieve power in an emergency.

Or it may be that the missing piece is the power of conscience, the ethical presumptions of the voters in a democracy. That is all right so long as we all have the same conscience in certain essential matters, and an instructed conscience, an organized and a consistent conscience not likely to be obscured by appeals to the passions, or diverted by the apparent demands of expediency. But if these conditions are fulfilled it should be remembered that one name for organized conscience is law.

There may therefore be some value in the conception of a law for all mankind which lies behind the particular laws made by particular sovereign bodies, however democratic. This may be the missing piece that we want. Indeed it is a conception towards which international lawyers today have been working, particularly when they placed crimes against humanity in the indictment at the Nuremberg trials. But there is, so it seems to me, one essential point in the idea of law, without which law is not law at all. It is not that law must be the command of a properly constituted sovereign body, it is not that law must be something to which secular penalties are necessarily attached as sanctions, it is that law is something you obey, as a matter of rule. Law must not be only a general line of conduct which our feelings normally commend, or a policy which at this moment we believe falls in with our sense of expediency. It must be a rule which we feel it our duty to obey, and consistently to obey. Now whether there can be such a rule, so it seems to me, depends ultimately on our conception of the nature of the universe. But to that point I shall return later.

III

THE OLD CONSTITUTION
AND THE NEW DEMOCRACY

'Persecution, oppression, and severity are banished, either by the wisdom of our laws, or the mildness of our manners. Humanity and civility are spread through the land, the love of liberty, which among Britons is closely connected with the love of their Country, watches with a jealous eye, the most minute deviations from the rules of our excellent constitution; and promises to transmit it unimpaired to our posterity.' Discourse on 'Public Virtues' preached before the University of Cambridge, November 5th, 1765 (Text 1, Pt. ii, part of verse 17, 'Love the Brotherhood'), from Discourses on Various Subjects, *by W. S. Powell, D.D., late Archdeacon of Colchester, and Master of St. John's College, Cambridge, 1776.*

BUT the idea of law can probably never return to its old place in the state and society. Blackstone is dead and deeply buried, Halifax the Trimmer and other of the old English classic political writers are unknown to many who might gain advantage from a better acquaintance with them and English traditions are being strangely forgotten; and last and most of all the constitution which our forefathers so earnestly believed in, toasted after so many dinners, celebrated with such pompous oratory and called the palladium of their liberties, has been reformed out of all knowledge. The old system of government in which it was believed that the division of power guaranteed men's freedom has been replaced by democracy, which we have been told means 'the concentration of power'. How much then of the old conception of law and of rights guaranteed by law can survive in a world which is so different to the world in which Blackstone wrote and the old constitution was venerated?

And one obvious reflection immediately intrudes itself. The old rights were, it was believed, granted to man by God, but it is at least difficult to believe in rights granted to human beings by God, if you do not believe in God. The idea of a universe for which laws have been prescribed by its Creator, depends, after all, largely on one's belief in a Creator. In a universe called into being by the chance combination of physical elements and given order by the blind forces of evolution the dominating power may be the will of man, or the forces chemical, biological, psychological or what you will which may be believed to control the will of man, but it cannot be a power outside men and the universe. Of course, there may be some other sanction for the moral law, the matter has been the subject of endless and important, and very difficult, philosophical speculation. But the whole question must be postponed, for it is necessary to take things in their proper historical order if we are to understand their significance, and the forces that destroyed that old world and created modern Britain were not inspired by a disbelief in God. In fact in England many, most, of the reformers were specifically, even self-consciously, Christian.

They had good reason for demanding reform. The law about which Blackstone wrote so complacently was, after all, very bad, it was full of absurd technicalities and unreason, beside the reasonably quick death of the gallows it prescribed for many the long lingering death in life of a suit in Chancery. The constitution in which Blackstone believed, and which was supposed to guarantee Englishmen's liberties, was largely a fraud, a splendid and useful fraud if you will, but a fraud nevertheless. It was supposed to be an elaborate system of checks and balances, the king was the executive part charged with government; the legislature was composed of king, lords and commons, that is the king in association with two bodies that represented different elements in the community; whilst the judges were carefully separated from royal influence by the provision of the Act of Settlement, and their power was restrained by the power of the jury. This division of power, so it was held, made tyranny impossible. But the difficulty was that if that division had been as absolute as theory demanded government would have been impossible too, and the answer that the eighteenth century had found was to glue king and legislature together, largely with the glue of corruption. The king's ministers purchased a majority in parliament by buying members of both houses. They could do this because the hunger for rewards, jobs, honours, pensions and the like was great and political morality low, but the task was made easier by the fact that the electorate which elected the house of commons was narrow, venal, arbitrary and absurd, providing a rich field for the resources of the Treasury. Consequently,

instead of power being divided it was to a large extent concentrated first in the hands of the ministers of the king, like Sir
Robert Walpole or the ineffable Duke of Newcastle, and later on
in the hands of the king himself, when that king was George III.

It is true that the power to be concentrated was limited. Local
authorities could do, very largely, as they liked. There was no
police system, Wesley could be dragged by his hair down the
streets of Wednesbury in Staffordshire by free-born Englishmen,
with whom no public authority interfered. The southern
counties could be terrorized by smugglers until Goodhurst in
Kent was forced to fight it out with them on its own. Riot, as
witness the riots against the restrictions on the sale of gin or the
removal of restrictions on Papists, was almost a constitutional
expedient. There was plenty of freedom, particularly for the
rough, the brutal and the strong. Nor was that freedom without
benefit to Englishmen. The legal protection which the system
offered to opponents of government was by no means illusory.
The judges protected Wilkes and his associates from George III;
the jury Horne Tooke, Thelwal and others from Pitt, at the time
of the panic of the French Revolution. Moreover the political
concentration of power was never complete. There were always
independent constituencies or constituencies in independent
ownership. There was always some opposition in the House of
Commons, and even an eighteenth-century parliament was not
deaf to the demands of public opinion when it was angry enough;
indeed, the remarkable fact is that the unreformed electorate was
representative enough in the end to elect the parliaments that
enabled the Whigs to pass the great Reform Act of 1832, which
abolished the worst constituencies and began the long, slow
pilgrimage from oligarchy to democracy.

But none of this is enough to vindicate the old constitution.
It was often oppressive enough. It was always oligarchical, it was
absurd, it would only work if its mechanism was richly lubricated
by the grease of corruption. Certainly it served its historical
purpose well, it carried England through the period of absolute
monarchies, taught her much about politics and prepared a
system of cabinet government which was greatly to assist the
development of practical democracy, but it was clearly right for
the men of the nineteenth century to clean it away and develop
a system of government which was more rational, and more
nearly represented government by the people.

But though what men have revolted against may excuse their actions, it is what they accept that will affect their future. Democracy was to be more than an alternative to old corrupt oligarchy, it was to be a positive creed. It might, or it might not, be informed by the spirit of Christianity, but its nature would certainly affect the way the Christian tradition survived. What differences was the change to make? The answer is, of course, very complicated, but one difference has already been suggested. The old constitution was supposed to be a balance of forces; the nineteenth century introduced into the system a force which could permit no balance or check against itself. With the development of the idea that the House of Commons represented the will of the people it came to seem to be more and more intolerable that there should be any check on that will. The change was slow, but it was in theory fundamental; for it affected the whole idea of the kind of object the constitution was to serve. The old idea of the constitution was as a framework for existing rights, it was to protect men in the enjoyment of what was their own, otherwise men would not have accepted, even in theory, so ponderous and ineffective a machine. It may be argued that the eighteenth century was peculiar in its respect for private rights, and certainly before the great civil war the king had much greater discretionary powers to impose his will, but even then, Englishmen would have revolted, and did revolt, at the idea that they held their own at the mercy of the king's will. But the new constitution was to become, in the last resort, in theory, not a framework for rights, but a vehicle for will. True, much of the equipment for protecting the individual remained, and remains. The independence of the judges survives, the jury survives to administer a law which is, in many ways, better than the law of the eighteenth century, but may not it be said, at the moment, that the primary object of the constitution is, at least in most men's minds, to secure that the will of the people shall prevail?

This indeed was a point which the Tories who opposed the Reform Bill of 1832 saw, confusedly and angrily, and they made a great deal of noise about it. The Bill would not only make Government impossible, it might not only lead to something like the French Revolution, it would also subordinate England to the representatives of one class, it would mean the subordination of the independence of the two branches of the legislation, the king and the lords, to the third, the House of Commons; and

one man, Mr. Holt Leigh, having the misfortune to die from an
excited mob whilst trying to cast his vote in 1831, in Wigan, sits
on his very dirty memorial in Leeds Parish Church holding on
his knees a carven book representing the British Constitution
being as it were a martyr for that cause.

But even if those Tories were prophetically and remotely right,
their words had no true relevance to contemporary issues. Even
before 1832, for all the system of checks and balances, the liberties
of men had often been at the mercy of one class, the class, or
party, or group, that controlled parliament; as Roman Catholics
and Dissenters and Radicals and the peasantry had all in turn
found to their cost. Nor for long after 1832 can it be said that the
will of the people prevailed to any devastating effect, certainly
not the will of the mass of the people. The electorate was only
democratized with becoming deliberation, the task being not
really effectively completed until 1884. The old classes still kept
their ancient places at the head of the community; and the new
liberal forces that struggled against them were apt to demand not
less freedom but more. It was a period not of too little freedom,
but of too much, too much freedom for the manufacturer, or the
owner of property which might be in jerry-built houses, vermin-
ous cellars or even in the filth that rotted and ripened in the streets.
Only after long debate and much delay did the state learn to take
to itself the powers which it was morally necessary for it to use
in order to ameliorate the lot of those for whom political liberty,
by itself, could mean nothing at all. Gradually parliament learned
to interfere in certain cases in the conditions of industry, but it
was only in the late 'sixties that public health really acquired, as
was said, 'the imperative mood', only in the 'seventies that steps
were taken to prepare a school for every child, and later still
before men were prepared to send every child to school. Indeed
it was left for the twentieth century to build at all comprehensively the 'social service state'.

Yet fundamental principles have a way of working themselves
out if there is nothing to divert them; moreover at times in
history excellent and necessary developments have led in the end
to questionable conclusions. The acceptance of democracy was
necessary, the creation of the social service state, with its health
services, its educational services, its insurance schemes, was
excellent. But the sequel is beginning to produce problems,
particularly for those who believe that man must not be the pawn,

since he is not, in the last resort, the creature, of the society in which he lives. For both are beginning to mean a greater concentration of coercive power in the hands of government.

That power is sometimes directly administrative. In order to make the social service state work at all, indeed in order to help the complicated community of modern times, diversified as it is by such things as the vagaries of the internal combustion engine and dealing in humans by the million, in some sort of liveable order, it is, as has been said, necessary to equip modern governments with far more complex discretionary powers than our rude forefathers ever dreamed of. This is done largely by equipping the ministers of the crown and other authorities with the power to make regulations that shall have the force of law, so that in many departments of life an Englishman no longer lives under the protection of a known and stable law, but under the compulsion of innumerable regulations, changing, developing, proliferating as the policy of the government develops, and telling him in not always very intelligible language what he must, or must not do.

Or that coercive power may be economic. In order to conquer industry for the good of the people it may be necessary for the people to own industry, or large parts of it, and the state may become the only available employer for large numbers of men and women, speaking with much greater force than could any private employer to the trade unions, or perhaps turning the trade unions into its own servants. Of course, the whole of that question is uncomfortably controversial; it is a matter of controversy how much the social service state will need to nationalize industry; it is a matter of controversy in what way that nationalization will effect the independence of those who are employed. But what is not controversial is that the social service state will cost money and that money must be raised by taxation from the rich, from the people of middling or small fortune and from everyone. Now that money will not be given to the poor, it will be spent for the benefit of the poor, which in terms of human freedom is not quite the same thing. Expenditure is the exercise of power, he who pays the piper calls the tune, and as a nightmare possibility there might come a time when there was in England only one great tune to which all must dance, because no one could afford pipe and tabor for himself.

Of course, on the other side it must be said that to attack

D

ignorance and ameliorate conditions is to extend freedom, that illiteracy and the proliferation of bed bugs are far worse enemies to human dignity than the proliferation of regulations; and that unemployment is the worst enemy of all. With all of which all men of goodwill would be agreed. Indeed most men of goodwill would be agreed on so much in this matter, that the discussion of the whole problem is always likely to tail off from the questions of principles into the problems of expediency, the problems of less or more, and whether it is really necessary to do this to secure that end, or whether something else really serves any useful purpose at all, problems with which in this book we can have nothing to do. But the problem of principle remains behind the problems of expediency, and should be considered by all parties. And the issue of principle seems to be this. The concentration of power is not the same as the distribution of liberty; in the last resort an element in liberty must be to conduct some part of your own life as you think fit, to have some part of you which is your own which the state not only will not, but may not, and cannot, take from you. Of course, there is no justification for this liberty being the monopoly, or at the mercy, of those to whose fingers wealth has adhered. Better be ruled, it may be said, by the will of all than the will of those who happen to have money to spend or can employ their fellows; but that consideration, for what it is worth, does not negative the fact that the will of all is not the same thing as the will of each and everyone.

Moreover it may be worth while to consider sometimes what in a democratic state the 'will of all' means. On the very largest issues, as for instance on the general determination to pursue the policy of social reform, one may take it that there is a general accord in the country. But on the particular points of policy, that matter so much, does the 'will of all' mean more than the will of the majority voting in rough-and-ready fashion at the last general election on some of the issues that then seemed to be important? Indeed it may not even mean the will of the majority, for a general election in Great Britain is by way of being a gamble and the strength of parties never accurately represents the distribution of opinion among the voters. More-over, it must mean the will of that majority, or minority, dis-tilled through the machinery of government touching issues of which electors have never heard, taking actions of which most of them will never hear, and could not possibly understand. It may be interpreted in the light of such things as the vanity of municipal officials or the overweening confidence of city fathers proud to represent the people after an election, at which, if they were very lucky, about half of the electorate voted. It is necessary to accept such things as the governing power in democracy since it is necessary to have some power that shall make decisions, and it is necessary to tolerate the fictions of a democracy because a democracy is so much more tolerable than any other form of government. But when it comes to an agreement about moral sanctions it is a good thing now and again to reconsider the title-deeds.

Of course, none of this means that the ideals suggested in the last chapter cannot survive. The idea of rights inherent in human beings guaranteed by the law of God can, indeed must, be maintained even when they can no longer be guaranteed by a balanced constitution or an ancient law. They must be written in the hearts of men. But the danger in England, at least at the moment, is not that essential rights will be consciously destroyed, but that the whole legacy of English freedom will be gradually whittled away, because no one has given sufficient thought to the problems involved. What we have to fear, to speak in terms of prehistoric animals, is not the sabre-toothed tiger, but the diplodocus, the vast creature with a small brain a very long way off and very heavy feet.

In particular it may be worth while to observe that even those things which have usually been thought necessary for the maintenance or propagation of Christianity may be whittled away. The state in England is not likely to become anti-Christian, at least not overtly, as far as can at the moment be foreseen. But it cannot now be specifically Christian. Christianity is a dogmatic creed, at least a good many people think it is, and the state, which draws its resources from everyone, ought not to use them to propagate controversial dogmatic opinion, or even, really, that absence of dogma which is a dogma in itself. Therefore, increasingly as existing endowments dry up, what is necessary for the ministrations of the Christian Church, churches, chapels, priests, ministers and above all schools, must be supported from pockets which the state is increasingly emptying to propagate its own views, or lack of view. The problem is a very difficult one, particularly when it concerns denominational teaching in schools, a shot-scarred battlefield which many people instinctively shun. But those who view that controversy with indifference bordering on disgust might consider whether teasing problems may not arise on issues not specifically religious, when the state has become chief paymaster of all letters, all science, and all art.

I do not wish to discuss these problems, I certainly do not want to try to suggest solutions, partly because I cannot see my way to any satisfactory theoretical solution, and partly because all that is important for present purposes is to point the difference in theory between a community based on a conception of elaborate guarantees for individual rights, however unequal, and a society whose practice seems increasingly to suggest the theory of a predominant will, however benevolent; an issue which must be considered, if the theory of inherent rights is an important part of the Christian tradition. However, one thing is certain, theory is not everything, law is not everything, they no more represent the whole state of society than a skeleton represents a whole living man. Other factors will always be at work to determine how the theory will work out, and what the law will be made to do. They will be material and spiritual. The economic practices and needs of society at any given moment will obviously always play an important part, but so will the literature that men read, the commonplaces they repeat, the habits they inherit, and above all, the whole social pattern they accept; and if men pretend to be Christians, Christianity will affect these things also.

Of course, it will always be a question how the pattern of the community, to which we must now turn, is moulded by Christianity, and how much that pattern controls what men think of Christianity; for in a Christian country each will always affect the other, though men will often believe they are taking the gospels unadulterated. But our forefathers were of the belief that there was an order in society which was derived directly from the providence of God, indeed they were of the belief that if it had not been for that providence there would have been no order at all. They were not agreed as to the nature of that order, indeed it is an important factor in the English heritage that there were important Christian groups who declined to accept an Established Church as part of that order. But before we consider Dissent, it is necessary to consider what they were dissenting from, and therefore in the next chapters it will be necessary to consider the essentials of what may be called the official order of society before we go on to the rebels.

Now that order necessarily changed a good deal in the course of history and since this is not a history book it will be best to think of it in its later stages, immediately before it was tossed about and confused by the powerful cross currents of the period of reform and revolution, for it is its latest form which is likely to influence us. We inherit from the seventeenth century, from the Tudors, from medieval England, from the Romans, or Saxons or Ancient Britons if you will, but we inherit through the eighteenth century; the eighteenth and nineteenth centuries have left their marks on all the goods that come to us. It may be held that this is unfortunate. It may be held that the century of the Beggar's Opera, of Sir Robert Walpole and Bubb Doddington is not very likely ground to search for a traditional moral order, and many will hold that the whole thing had been stubbed up before that age, that the Reformation had destroyed the discipline of the Church, that the English Revolution and the power of capital had swept away such moral control as the Tudor and Stuart state had put in its stead, that rationalism had reduced the predominance of religion, and nothing was left but the insolence of private property and the growing power of ruthless commerce. Certainly if that was the whole truth it is difficult to see that we could inherit anything direct from a past which had become in such sort empty, swept and garnished. But it is not the whole truth. In the eighteenth century England was still a Christian country with a traditional pattern of social morality, a fact to which the bishop in his pulpit, or the wretch who made his last dying confession at Tyburn, were both willing to testify; and from that pattern we have inherited more than we are ready to believe. To that then we must turn, with now and again a glance over our shoulder at previous centuries since what we are to think about was already an ancient inheritance.

IV

THE OLD ORDER OF SOCIETY—
SECULAR

'Answer. My duty towards my neighbour is to love him as myself, and to do to all men as I would they should do unto me: To love, honour, and succour my father and mother: To honour and obey the King, and all that are put in authority under him: To submit myself to all my governors, teachers, spiritual pastors and masters: To order myself lowly and reverently to all my betters: To hurt nobody by word nor deed: To be true and just in all my dealing: To bear no malice nor hatred in my heart: To keep my hands from picking and stealing, and my tongue from evil speaking, lying and slandering. To keep my body in temperance, soberness, and chastity: Not to covet or desire other men's goods: but to learn and labour truly to get mine own living, and to do my duty in that state of life, unto which it shall please God to call me.' The Catechism in the Book of Common Prayer.

SIR JOHN ELIOT, the great Parliamentary leader, speaking in the House of Commons in 1625, called attention to the excitement which always developed there when the question of religion came up. 'It is observable', said he, 'in the House of Commons as their whole story gives it, that wherever that mention does break forth of the fears and dangers in religion and the increase of popery their affections are much stirred; and whatever is obnoxious to the state it then is reckoned as an incident to that.'[1] This was of course only to be expected in that conscience-troubled seventeenth century. The storm which the reformation had let loose on the world was still high—a religious Armageddon had actually broken out in Germany—and there was turmoil in the minds of Englishmen. Religion was the deepest intellectual interest of very many men and women, and was also the robe in which secular politics and secular interests were most normally draped; while those who expounded religion or engaged in religious controversy were very many indeed. Whether the Lord had given the Word or no, certainly the company of the preachers was great.

But behind Eliot's speech was an idea which had existed before that spiritual turmoil and which outlasted it. To continue with

[1] John Forster, *Sir John Eliot: A Biography*, 1864, Vol. I, p. 245.

what he said at that time on the importance men attached to religion, 'Religion is that which keeps the subject in obedience as being taught by God to honour His Vice-gerents. *A religando it is called* as the common obligation among men; the tie of all friendship and society; the bond of all office and relation; writing every duty in the conscience which is the strictest of all laws.'[1] Now the first sentence of that quotation may have a foreign, indeed a questionable ring for us. The idea that a proper object of religion is to keep anyone in subjugation may well seem to a modern reader to be an obvious prostitution of Christianity for doubtful secular purposes, the kind of purposes which a modern reader finds it easy to sum up and dismiss, without much further consideration, under the comprehensive heading of the 'doctrine of the Divine right of Kings'. But Eliot was no supporter of Stuart pretensions. He was indeed one of the most courageous leaders of the opposition to Charles I, and died in prison a martyr for the cause of parliamentary liberty.

In fact Eliot's statement was the expression of what was a generally accepted commonplace both to the men of his own generation and to many in those which succeeded it. It is true that it was a commonplace which came home poignantly to the men of the sixteenth and seventeenth centuries, partly because it touched on a common fear. The conception of order was deep rooted in the philosophy of the sixteenth and seventeenth centuries, it is evident in the writings of Hooker, and as scholars have pointed out it is present in Shakespeare's plays.[2] But it was never only a philosophical conception, it was a matter of urgent day-to-day need. In a world when men went armed and were not easily governed, when civil war and armed rebellion and plots and treasons filled most of the pages of recent history, the needs for order, for subjecting the unruly wills and affections of sinful men to some power that could maintain peace, seemed to be a matter of pressing necessity. Order must be prayed for continually, it must be inculcated with all the force at command; and the power that should do the work was clearly doing the work of God, and was God's vice-gerent on earth.[3]

[1] Forster, *op. cit.*, Vol. I, p. 248.

[2] See E. M. W. Tillyard, *Shakespeare's History Plays*, London 1944, and *Elizabethan World Picture*, London 1943.

[3] See J. W. Allen, *A History of Political Thought in the Sixteenth Century*, London 1928, Part II, Ch. II, 'The Doctrine of Non-Resistance', pp. 125 *ff.*

You can find the sentiment in the homilies of the Church of England in which rebellion is spoken of as the 'whole Puddle and Sink of all sins against God and man'.[1] You can find it in the Book of Common Prayer where 'privy conspiracy and rebellion' is placed in the Litany as one of the evils from which deliverance is sought, associated with 'plague, pestilence and famine' and most significantly with 'false doctrine, heresy and schism'. You can find it in the curious sermons which Bishop Andrewes composed on the 'Gowrie Conspiracy'. Of course in the prayers of the Established Church, and in the teaching of its divines, you have the words of a portion of the Church very closely connected with secular authority and for every reason anxious to support it. But that anxiety was not only the anxiety of ecclesiastics to support the power that endorsed the type of ecclesiastical organization in which they believed, it was also a deep anxiety for order in a potentially very disorderly world, which was indeed one of the reasons why they believed that ecclesiastical organization had been instituted. The feeling is strange to us, since in our modern highly organized and artificial society we are apt to take for granted many of the elementary necessities of organized life of which our forefathers did not feel secure; but it may well be that the future will prove that in this we are wrong.

It was a matter of faith that God had established the pattern of this much desired order in His plan for mankind. Of course the nature of that pattern or plan was a matter of controversy. The Roman Catholic or the Presbyterian had a very different picture in their mind from that of the Anglican, Sir John Eliot no doubt a very different view of the rights of God's vice-gerents from that of High Churchmen like Mainwaring and Montague, or even Archbishop Laud. Given a divinely ordained authority, it was natural to believe that it was the type of authority which would endorse what oneself valued; and as the English Church struggled into self-consciousness as a special and distinctive portion of the Catholic Church claiming continuity with the old, but also claiming to be reformed, it was natural that it should lean heavily on the royal power that fostered, governed and protected it. In a world in which on every side strident voices were claiming to command in the name of Christ, independence

[1] 'The Third Part of the Homily against Disobedience and Wilful Rebellion,' XXXIII, Certain Sermons or Homilies appointed to be read in Churches, ed. 1683, p. 365. See also X, 'An Exhortation to Obedience'.

of action, freedom to do what seemed necessary and right could only be secured by power which could also cite no lesser authority to endorse its actions. It was natural therefore for the English Church, fighting for its existence in a war of two fronts against Papist and Presbyterian, to emphasize the divine origin of the monarch's authority. For both Papist and Presbyterian were at least agreed in this. They believed that Christ had instituted a Church which was endowed with a right to command the secular authority, even were he a king, to impose its own religious pattern on society, and, if necessary, to use for that purpose the sword of persecution.

Therefore as the seventeenth-century struggle deepened and extended it was inevitable that doctrines about the divine rights of kings should become the centre of controversy. They served their purpose for both good and ill. They helped to secure the continued existence of an ecclesiastical system which probably after some sort was that which most Englishmen came to prefer, they also probably helped on occasion to subordinate religion to the needs of secular politics. They helped to prevent the subjection of England to sectarian tyranny, they were also responsible for repression and persecution, and at times threatened liberties which most Englishmen cherished. For members of the Church of England their sense and use was destroyed when the sovereign became a Roman Catholic and, so it appeared to them, went about to destroy what he ought to defend. In the eighteenth century they were left behind by an age in which in truth they were no longer necessary, since political demands were no longer urged in the name of Christ with a hotch-potch of texts to back them up, but rather in the name of reason, or nature, or utility, so that the full belief in the hereditary divine rights of kings remained only alive among those men who, tragic or ridiculous, whichever you will, were prepared to throw wealth, honour, lands away for an obsolete ideal with 'vain faith and courage vain'. But the important thing is that there remained in the minds of many Englishmen long after Jacobitism had turned into a romantic memory a pattern of order in the state, which was older than the crisis of the Reformation and survived the English Revolution, and which has left a very deep mark on the English tradition.

In 1712 that subtle philosopher and good Christian George Berkeley, afterwards Bishop of Cloyne, preached three common-places in the chapel of Trinity College, Dublin, to inculcate the importance of 'Passive obedience, or, the Christian doctrine of not resisting the supreme power'. These he worked up into a discourse which is in many ways a typically eighteenth-century production, for the case is, as the title says, 'Proved and vindicated upon the principles of the Law of Nature', and not upon the catena of texts by which an earlier writer might have hoped to invoke scriptural authority for an order established by direct divine legislation. But the motives are not new. There is, indeed, still the old fear of disorder. 'The miseries', Berkeley says, 'inescapable from a state of anarchy are easily imagined. So insufficient is the wit or strength of any single man, either to avert the evils, or to procure the blessings of life and so apt are the wills of different persons to contradict and thwart each other, that it is absolutely necessary, several independent powers be combined together, under the direction (if I may so speak) of one and the same will, I mean the law of the society. Without this there is no politeness, no order, no peace among men, but the world is one great heap of misery and confusion, the strong as well as the weak, the wise as well as the foolish, standing on all its sides exposed to all those calamities, which man can be liable to in a state where he has no other security than the not being possessed of anything which may raise envy or desire in another.'[1]

From this he deduced that submission to the supreme authority has a necessary connection with the well-being of the whole sum of mankind and is a 'moral duty or branch of natural religion'. This submission, however, was taught with special force and particularity by Christianity. In his *Discourse to Magistrates*, which he produced later in his life, he says, 'Every religion that inculcates virtue and discourages vice, is for the public benefit. The Christian religion doth not only this, but further makes any legal constitution sacred by commanding submission thereto. "*Let every soul be subject to the higher power*", saith St. Paul, "*for the powers that be are ordained of God*".' It was therefore wise, according to Berkeley, that the Christian religion should be 'established by law; and so established, and wrought into the very frame and principles of our government, is become a main part of the civil constitution'.[2]

The language may be different, but the conception is not far

---

[1] *The Works of George Berkeley, D.D., Late Bishop of Cloyne in Ireland*, London 1784, Vol. II, pp. 14, 15.

[2] *Berkeley's Works, op. cit.*, Vol. II, pp. 300 and 313.

removed from that of Sir John Eliot, it is that of a community controlled and ordered by the Christian conscience. Men must obey, and it is better for them to obey for conscience sake than for wrath; but the sole use of conscience is not to make subjects obedient. Conscience is to bind ruler as well as subject. 'It is indeed', says Berkeley, 'a breach of the law of nature for a subject though under the greatest and most unjust sufferings to lift up his hand against the supreme power. But it is a more heinous and inexcusable violation of it, for the persons invested with the supreme power to use that power to the ruin and destruction of the people committed to their charge.'[1] Or again: 'It is manifest that no prince upon earth can hope to govern well, or even to live easy and secure, much less respected by his people, if he do not contribute by his example and authority to keep up in their minds an awful sense of religion.'[2] Even princes, then, must do their duty in that state of life, unto which it shall please God to call them.

Now Berkeley was possibly unusual in teaching passive obedience, in an age when many men followed the philosopher, Locke, and believed in a revocable social contract, indeed his sermon laid him open to the unmerited charge of Jacobitism. But his sense of the dangers that might threaten the order of society was by no means unique: you will find it for instance in a plea made by Isaac Watts, the celebrated Dissenter, for the support of Charity schools;[3] indeed it might have occurred naturally to any man who watched the faces in the eighteenth-century streets, if Hogarth is any guide. Still less was Berkeley unique in his century in his conception of a society controlled and maintained by the sanctions of religion. Indeed the main thesis of that famous eighteenth-century work, Bishop Warburton's *Divine Legation of Moses Demonstrated*, is based on the proposition that the inculcation of the doctrine of a future state of rewards and punishments is necessary to the well-being of civil society, a theme which Warburton elaborates with much curious learning and some rather curious argument.

Warburton also was not solely concerned with religion as the guardian of the order of society. While developing his theme he makes the perfectly sound point that there are certain important

[1] *Ibid.*, Vol. II, p. 33.
[2] *Ibid.*, Vol. II, p. 301.
[3] Isaac Watts, D.D., *Sermons, Discourses and Essays*, sect., 1753, pp. 723 *ff.*

duties which the state cannot enforce and which must necessarily be imposed on society by the sanctions of religion. These duties were generally recognized in the eighteenth century. They spread out from the primary duties of a man to his family, and they rested on every man in his station, on the poor man to get his own living and to do his duty or 'sarvice' whatever that might be, on the educated man with greater force than on the uneducated because of his greater chance of knowing what was required, and on the noble, the magistrate, and the rich man to fulfil the duties of their station in life.

But here perhaps it is best to turn to another great eighteenth-century philosopher and divine. In 1740 Bishop Butler, preaching before the corporation of London, told his audience: 'In short, he who has distributed men into these different ranks, and at the same time united them into one society, in such sort as men are united, has, by this Constitution of things, formally put the poor under the superintendency and patronage of the rich. The rich then are charged, by natural providence, as much as by revealed appointment with the care of the poor.'[1] Here again the sentiment expressed was a commonplace, you would probably only have to study a selection of the other 'charity' sermons in which that century abounded to find it re-echoed by a great variety of divines from a great many different pulpits.

The old picture of society was therefore that of a community whose order depended upon the will of God and which needed the sanctions of religion to make organized life possible. In that order every man had his station and each station its peculiar responsibilities which the commands of God straightly enjoined and the justice of God would strictly enforce, and it is possible that from that conception derives a very important factor in the national inheritance which combines easily with the legal factor and the results of self-government but is separate from it. I mean the strong sense of personal responsibility and of personal duty which can still be found among Englishmen.

If so, the nature of the legacy is very important. But is it so? There may be reason to doubt. In fact, three objections might be urged against the probability of England having in this matter inherited anything of real moral value from this tradition, at least through the unreformed eighteenth century. The first

---

[1] *The Works of Joseph Butler*, edited by the Right Hon. W. E. Gladstone, Oxford 1896, Vol. II, p. 305.

might be produced by the historian. He might say that before the eighteenth century a society, which was in some sort controlled by a moral order, had indeed existed, but that it had been destroyed. The work of the Reformation, the destruction of the old monarchy by the forces of a Parliamentary oligarchy of rich men, the triumph of capitalism and of various types of 'individualism', a word of vague content but as is usually considered now of damning effect, had swept away the moral discipline of society leaving only in its place the insolent rule of the wealthy. The second might be that of the modernist who might hold that all the social conceptions of any age which accepted the unequal distribution of wealth, must necessarily be so morally defective that no good could be inherited from them. The third might be that of the practical man who might with some reason ask whether these fine words had any effect on any one's actions, or whether they merely represented an official theory tepidly accepted but never markedly observed.

The first objection might indeed at the outset be grounded on the nature of these 'charity' sermons themselves. The word 'charity' has, since its use by those who translated 1 Cor. xiii, achieved a rather equivocal reputation, it is a partially fallen angel; for it has often represented neither that love which regards not self but only service, nor that service which a law demands whether there be love or not, but something betwixt and between, and something with which an amalgam of baser metal has often been mixed, altruism combined with a sense of patronage, a sense of obligation, obedience to which yields too much self-congratulation; and it may be that the partial disgrace of this word represents the change which had already taken place in the English tradition by the beginning of the eighteenth century.

It would not, if one cared for the truth, really be easy to affirm with any confidence that there was more love available in medieval or sixteenth-century England than in the eighteenth century: indeed the savagery, the cruelty, the social oppression in the record should make such an assertion impossible. But the sense of definite obligation may have been sharper before the last quarter or half of the seventeenth century. In a simpler, smaller, more traditional England, perhaps the particular duties on the shoulders of each particular member of society were clearer, and further than that, were matters which could be enforced by the sanction of hell-fire or of the law of the Church or the Star

Chamber, rather than by appeals to a benevolence which may be near neighbour to vanity. But long before the eighteenth century began England had largely shaken off effective ecclesiastical discipline, in 1641 the coercive power of Star Chamber and Council, which had been used on occasion to keep men up to their social duty, had been broken for ever, in the seventeenth century the ethical background had been pierced and torn by religious individualism, and perhaps the way made the clearer for the all-mastering forces of commerce and trade. Therefore, in eighteenth-century England it might be said that it had come to be the habit of preachers and theologians not to define and to rail and to damn, which are the proper tasks for theologians or preachers, but to be polite and to commend and to appeal, which are not quite the same things.

Such is the historical objection. But on closer inspection it would seem to be both unsatisfactory and elusive. It should be remembered that generalizations about changes in the moral climate are always difficult to make, and normally unsatisfactory when made, since it is very difficult to cover all the evidence that should be relevant. The point on which one touches firmest ground is the political point. Certainly the Council, with the Star Chamber to back it, had on occasion forced upon men a higher standard of social conduct than they would otherwise have adopted, or probably desired. It is also true that in the eighteenth century the laws which had been passed to control conditions of labour, wages, prices and the like, that is, the economic duties and rights of each man in his station, were apt to fall into disuse, and the opinion seems to have gained ground that it served no useful purpose to try to interfere by government regulation with the operations of economic forces, a feeling not always shared, strange to say, by those for whose presumed benefit these regulations had been framed. But the process was piecemeal and never uniform or complete. Human nature abhorred the moral vacuum of the completely *laissez-faire* state, and at the time that the last of the old laws were repealed the first of the new factory acts were being tried. Moreover it would seem that the change in the practice of the state was more the result of a change in economic opinion and of practical organization than the result of a universal change in social morality, and that the old regulations were less philanthropic in object and the new freedom less morally indifferent in practice than one might at first sight believe. Certainly the discussions of magistrates and members of parliament about the state of the poor at the end of the eighteenth century do not seem to suggest that men had by that time lost all count of their social duties in this matter. But such comparisons are difficult, and I am not capable of making them, and I would content myself with saying that in the eighteenth century the belief that each man in his station had particular duties towards his neighbours seems to have been widely enough accepted to have made it possible for us to have inherited an important tradition through them.

But then comes the second objection. Was not that tradition so morally defective that anything inherited from it must be an encumbrance? After all, Bishop Butler's idea that God had put the poor under the superintendency and patronage of the rich is not an idea that would win much modern approval. Of course he spoke the language of his time. His was a world which accepted without question a hierarchical society with a well-defined system of classes. That idea at least was not new, indeed the idea that society was permanently divided into rich and poor, gentle and simple, was so old that it seemed to be part of nature, and was indeed the historic mould into which Christian morality had been poured. But we may well hold that we have learnt to think more finely than that, that we cannot accept a permanent hereditary inequality of opportunity and advantage, and that we must reject anything that comes to us with the stamp of that mould upon it as morally counterfeit.

It would, however, be as well not to be too hasty in taking up that attitude. Moral contempt for the values of the past is normally foolish, sometimes disastrous and always ignorant. After all it is due to no virtue of ours that we believe in a more equal society, we have inherited that belief largely from the thought of the nineteenth century; and we have not yet succeeded in putting it into effect. When expelled from the front door inequality and privilege have shown a regrettable tendency to come in again furtively by the back window, and apart from that there is one point which we can learn with advantage from the old tradition.

In the older conception with all its defects a direct personal responsibility lay inescapably on the shoulders of the individual. That is not always true in the modern conception. In the modern conception most things must necessarily be done by the state. Most services will be performed by professional servants paid for by taxpayers who have no choice. The moral responsibility is indefinitely diffused, and the exponent of the system may be claiming moral prestige for advocating services which other men will perform, for which other men will pay but from which he may benefit. From the point of utility no doubt he may be right in his advocacy, but it may not seem to be a legitimate cause for spiritual pride.

But the third objection remains behind. To what extent, then, was the old idea of social duty ever a reality? To what extent was it not simply an ideal enjoined with much thumping of the pulpit cushion, which did not really affect men's actions in the real world where men quarrelled, lusted and oppressed, and the poor suffered? The question is a very important one, but it is a very difficult one to answer. It is difficult even if, to make it more practicable, we confine it to the eighteenth century. Of course in the eighteenth century there are very heavy items on the debit side. There was much profligacy, callous brutality and cruelty in that century with, it would seem, an ugly speciality in indecent blasphemy such as one seldom comes across nowadays. Both Bishops Butler and Berkeley deplore much that they find in that world; in fact Berkeley's address to magistrates is, so he says in the title, 'occasioned by the enormous License and Irreligion of the Times'.

Now these things disgraced men in every rank in society. As one travels through eighteenth-century England with Smollett or Fielding or even Fanny Burney one meets some singularly unattractive types; the satyr, the fop, the local tyrant, the bully and the blackguard, and where these men have social position they use it frankly to further their own evil ends. Nor does society provide more than sporadic and casual protection for their victims. Of course novelists must have villains, but there is enough to be found in the records to prove that these figures are not wholly untrue to life. Moreover, in addition to the blackguards there is the mass of the relatively indifferent, men who accepted the privileges of their position and did not exercise themselves very much about their duties to the less fortunate. The half-animal country gentleman whose thoughts did not stray very far from his partridges, his hounds and his bottle, the enclosing landlord who did not much regard the rights of his neighbour, the prosperous farmer who used his position in the parish to keep down the poor rate, the great noble or grandee who used all he could lay his hands on to engage in the corrupt game of politics, or to build at vast expense a great country palace, all these men were like to use their station in society for their own ends and none of them to be much impeded in doing what they wanted by their duty to others. And to these one must add the absentee parson, the clerical pluralist and the negligent bishop.

Yet there is also much on the credit side. For one thing it is important to realize how much public work in the eighteenth century was done voluntarily, with no reward, but as a matter of duty and with a strong sense of social responsibility, sometimes limited, sometimes very enlightened. It is clear that many of the clergy, the nobility and the gentry, and other rich men in the eighteenth century, felt some of that sense of duty towards their poorer neighbours which in prevalent theory they ought to have felt. Of course the extent of their action varied widely from individual to individual. At the one end of the scale you have a saintly person like Lady Betty Hastings who lived a life almost completely devoted to piety and the service of mankind in the great house at Ledstone in Yorkshire, and who devoted a con- siderable proportion of her large property to founding schools and endowing scholarships. At the other end you might place some dull country-gentleman whose duty to the poor was perhaps restricted to ordering poor relief to those whose lot chance might bring to his notice, and perhaps leaving some small pro- vision in his will to provide red flannel for the poor old women of his parish. But it is worth while to recognize that while the crimes and the failures of the eighteenth century are many and glaring, its charities, the charity schools, the orphanages and alms houses and particularly the infirmaries and the hospitals and dis- pensaries occupy an important place in the history of the human- ization of society in England. And many of these were at least in part prompted by the idea that rank, office, property or even residence in a neighbourhood imposed particular obligations on men and women.

In fact the old conception of the moral order of society was not without its practical results, and in spite of what may have happened in the sixteenth century and seventeenth century it remained a continuous tradition maintained in its own fashion in the eighteenth century and handed on as a living tradition to the nineteenth. Indeed in the nineteenth century it still flourished. It appears for instance in that typical product of the nineteenth

E

century, the improving landlord. You can see its results in nineteenth-century politics, and it is perhaps demonstrated at its best in the lives of such men as Sidney Herbert, Lord Frederick Cavendish or Lord John Manners. In private life it was largely responsible for much of the very valuable voluntary work done by men and still more by women of all classes, while nineteenth-century literature is full of it, in simple form in a book like *Ministering Children*, but more intelligently in the novels, as in the life, of Charlotte M. Yonge.

And anyone who knows England will know well that the remnants of that tradition are a living force today. We may no longer teach that the powers that be are ordained of God, nor are we impressed as profoundly as were our forefathers by the feeling that the sanctions of religion are necessary for the maintenance of any orderly life, perhaps because centuries of orderly life have led us to take internal peace for granted. We are suspicious of privilege, perhaps rather contemptuous of social eminence, though snobbery still exercises its mysterious force among us. What is still more important, we have had to equip the country with professional services which in many cases has made voluntary work irrelevant. The squire's daughters no longer teach in the village school, partly because the squire may have been taxed out of existence, but also because their place has certainly been taken by professional schoolmistresses who will teach the children very much better, and with greater regularity. But there are still many people in all classes in the country doing what they conceive to be the duties of their position, and whether they are valuable anachronisms or no, we cannot afford to abandon the central point of the old theory.

Eliot said that religion wrote every duty in the conscience because it was the strictest of all laws, innumerable divines said that it is better to obey for conscience sake than for wrath, and in spite of the claptrap of which our forefathers could on occasion be guilty, the old theory envisaged something of real moral value, a community in which men were bound together not by fear, not by habit, not by enlightened self-interest but by something more worthy of human beings, by conscience. We cannot afford to lose that bond. Without that bond both the general morality and the general humanity of the country would decrease, for Warburton was quite right in believing that no state can compel all the duties that must be performed to secure the proper conduct of humane and civilized life, and it cannot pay men to do them all either. Without that bond you cannot secure the necessary sense of personal responsibility, and without that bond England would not be England.

But the old order was by no means only philosophical or ethical, it was also strongly institutional and among the most important institutions of pre-nineteenth century England was one which had always been considered to be an organic part of the Christian order of society, and whose duty it was always considered to be to instruct men's consciences; I mean the Christian Church. To that Church I must turn, or rather without daring or desiring to start a controversy as to what the Christian Church is, or in what body at any point in English History to be found, I must turn to the Church of England as lawfully established in these realms in the last centuries of the old order.

V

THE OLD ORDER OF SOCIETY—
ECCLESIASTICAL

*'They all lived and died worthy members of the Church and firmly attached
to the true Protestant Interest of the Kingdom as by Law Established.'
Memorial to members of the Hitch family in Leathley Church, Yorkshire.*

FROM primitive times religious institutions seem to have
been woven inextricably into the warp and woof of human
organization. The primitive community, living for centuries in
the presence of its dead and its traditional holy places, and guided
by custom, may seem infinitely remote from our world in which
so many people live in communities which are urban and fluid
and without local or any other traditions. Yet from that root
much human organization may have developed by gradual
degrees with new elements continually being grafted into something which was already alive. Indeed the primitive elements
may not have been changed so rapidly or so completely as the
innovators believed.

Certainly, from very early medieval times, the priest in the
parish and the bishop high in the hierarchy of the nation had
been organic parts of the fabric of society. No doubt the Reformation made a very great difference, the links with the authority
of Rome were shattered; the frontier, the always disputed and
uncertain frontier, between what was under secular and what
under purely ecclesiastical control, was pushed far over to include
most, or it might be all, of the ecclesiastical territory. The power
of ecclesiastical law to control laymen was progressively reduced;
the monasteries disappeared and lay impropriors of tithe and
lay patrons of livings were multiplied exceedingly. Yet, whatever
the doctrinal implications of this change, the rapidity of its social
and political results can be exaggerated; the priest still remained
in the parish, if he was resident; indeed to judge from some of
the lists of incumbents it was through many of the startling
changes of the sixteenth century curiously often the same priest.

The bishop also remained high in the hierarchy of the nation, though after the Edwardian bishops had been burnt alive by the Roman Catholics, it was not, rather naturally, the same bishop. It is true that his purely political and secular functions were progressively reduced, but they did not disappear. In the first half of the eighteenth century the Archbishop of Canterbury was still made a member of the nominal Cabinet. All through the eighteenth century the bishops took their duties in the House of Lords very seriously.[1] In fact, the Church, still traditionally organized, still remained an intrinsic part of English society. In appearance, in form, in many surviving habits of mind and practice, if not, after the Civil War, in reality, England still retained the conception which Richard Hooker represented when he said: 'With us one society is both the Church and commonwealth.'[2]

In fact, on any reading of history that traditional organization had been too little disturbed. In one sense the Church of England was never reformed till the nineteenth century. In the sixteenth century, in the earliest stages of the work of the Reformation Parliament, a statute against pluralities had been passed, but so many exceptions had been introduced into it as to make it a sham, and the work of clearing up the abuses of the middle ages had never been attacked as it would have been if the work had fallen into the hands of more drastic Protestant reformers, or remained under Rome and become subject to the decrees of the council of Trent. The eighteenth- and nineteenth-century English clergy were as a body better educated than their predecessors in the fifteenth; they were probably more moral. But the administrative abuses, such things as the holding of two quite incompatible offices by the same man, the clerical sinecures and the rest of them, had survived and had got worse, and were as ever exploited by men to whom the Church was the source of wealth, the natural resource of the younger sons of the gentry and aristocracy, and not the sphere of duty.[3]

It is beyond the compass of this book to try to calculate the effect of these abuses, or to go further and try to assess the results of the ministrations of the parochial clergy in the life of the nation

[1] Rev. Norman Sykes, M.A., D.Phil., *Church and State in England in the Eighteenth Century*, Cambridge 1934, Ch. 2.

[2] Hooker, *Ecc. Pol.*, VIII, i, 7, Works Ed., Oxford 1865, Vol. II, p. 493.

[3] Norman Sykes, *op. cit.*, pp. 147–88.

either in the eighteenth or after the reform of standards in the nineteenth century. These are indeed matters in which all generalizations are suspect, particularly when they are provided, as they often have been in the past, to serve the purposes of a party, either political or ecclesiastical. Recent work has been more scholarly and in particular has served partly to dissipate some of the facile condemnations which have been passed on the Church in the eighteenth century.[1] But there is much that is important and significant that no historical research can ever recover. Men can suggest, but they can never know what has been the effect on English character of the constant repetition of the beautiful and reticent services of the Prayer Book of the English Church, of the emphasis on the ten commandments even intruded into the Church's most sacred service, of the constant reading of the Bible, or of the emphasis on order and the claims of the secular authority. They may with much labour give some idea of clerical assiduity or indolence, but they must leave us to speculate on what is the really important thing, that is, what was the real lasting influence of these men from holy Mr. Herbert, through men like Parson Woodforde to the outrageous and grotesque characters who sometimes appear in the records.

Certainly, the parson and his wife and his family have played a very considerable part in the history of the country; how great can sometimes be guessed from a journey through the English countryside. In village after village that the traveller passes there is the parish church, and there is the parsonage, often now called 'the old Rectory' or 'Vicarage', since it is too large for the resources of the present incumbent. But still the traveller can look over the gate and guess what it was in Victorian times; the croquet lawn, the drawing room where meetings were held, the nursery from the like of which so many remarkable men and women have come, and the vicar's study with the Arundel prints. But he must remember the prosperity these imaginations suggest had in many cases not always existed, was never universal, and probably now exists no more, though the parish priest, whatever his resources, is often still confidently expected to play a surprisingly large part in the community, even by those who never go near his church on Sundays.

Or the traveller could go into the church and read the epitaphs of those who while they lived haply worshipped there:

[1] Sykes, *op. cit.* See in particular pp. 1–7.

Their name, their years, spelt by th' unletter'd Muse,
The place of fame and elegy supply;
And many a holy text around she strews,
That teach the rustic moralist to die.

Yet even where, as indeed is normal, the muse is not so unlettered as Gray suggests, she is not much more communicative.
The faces are turned away from us, and the hearts are hidden.
We can never know to what extent those virtues were truly
practised, which are often so freely ascribed at least to those who
before the equalization of death were in the higher social ranks,
or how deeply those holy texts were believed. Something, of
course, can be gained from diaries, letters, works of devotion,
or the imaginative reconstruction by novelists such as Sterne,
Goldsmith, Fielding, Jane Austen, Charlotte Brontë, Charlotte
Yonge, George Eliot, Trollope, Samuel Butler and Thomas
Hardy. But what can be recovered is after all but a fragment of
a fragment of what is lost. How well, or how badly the clergy of
the Church of England did their work, and what its results were,
can in large part be known only to their Master. There, no doubt,
many of them would be content to let the matter rest. But it is
important that from time to time the historian should recognize
the limitations of his art, and recognize how doubtful and
ignorant are his generalizations about matters which have meant
very much in the formation of the national character.

Of course many generalizations could be attempted; it would
be possible to talk about robust commonsense, an emphasis on
practical morality, an avoidance of extremes, and except under
the influence of the Evangelical revival, a certain fear of emotion.
It would be difficult to say with confidence how universal these
traits have been, nor, where they seem to correspond, as they do,
with outstanding national characteristics, to be certain how largely
these have been the legacy of other historical factors than the
tradition of the Church of England. Yet however great is the
good which this country has inherited from the practice of the
Church of England, and it is probably very great, one generalization to the disadvantage of that Church must be made. It was an
Established Church. The ill effects of its relation to the state in
the possible pollution of its dogma can perhaps be exaggerated.
Indeed it is possible to make the case that it owes something of its
catholicity in dogma to this very fact, which has prevented one

ecclesiastical party from gaining control at any time and completely expelling the others. In 1854 Frederick Temple said: 'But I believe the true spiritual hold of the Church to reside in her non-discipline. The Church is now the most tolerant of all denominations; but she owes this characteristic to her bondage.'[1]

There was, however, another form of pollution. It was caused partly no doubt by the fact that in the eighteenth century as before the Reformation promotion could too often be gained by political favour and political services.[2] But it came, at least equally, from the influence of the private patron. Indeed the identification of the Church with the government of the country was perhaps not so morally dangerous, nor so habitual, as its too close identification with the governing classes of the country. The fact that good preferment was apt to go to the well connected, that it was too often mainly a satisfactory provision for younger sons, that the squire and the parson were often too closely allied, that the parson himself as tithe owner and glebe holder might be a man of property, that his education, his standing in society, might cause him to be considered to be a gentleman and therefore as something different from his parishioners: all these things helped to divide the Church of England from many whom it was its duty to serve, might make it neglect them, or only deal with them after a condescending fashion that was rightly resented by independent minds, a sentiment that has left deep marks on our inheritance.

It was, of course, the penalty exacted for the part the Church played in the social order. It can be exaggerated. Conditions were always very different in different parts of the country and there were always many clergymen who were obviously of humble origin socially, as there were many also who were very poor. Moreover in many cases and for long periods a social difference between the clergyman and his parishioners was rather valued than resented, it was part of the natural ordering of society and far more indignation was likely to be excited by the appointment of someone who was not a 'gentleman' than of someone who was. Still it was a potential source of evil which undoubtedly produced evil. It identified the Church of England too closely with the social and political interests of one class, an alliance which

[1] *Memoirs of Archbishop Temple by Seven Friends*, edited by E. G. Sandford, 1906, Vol. I, 274.

[2] Sykes, *Church and State in the Eighteenth Century*, p. 147.

could be typified perhaps by some of the activities of the clerical magistrates in the late eighteenth and early nineteenth centuries, by the alliance between many sections of the Church and first the Tory then the Conservative Party in the period of change that followed the French Revolution. This alliance might be perhaps defended by saying that at that time the Church was attacked, as also was the view of society for which the Church stood. But alliance of the Church with any political party is always danger-ous, it normally leads to the prostitution of spiritual influence, or of what ought to be spiritual influence. Moreover this alliance was not only one of ideas; it was one based on social affinities and common economic interests, as might perhaps be illustrated by the story of Tom Mosley about the silly curate of Keble, who burst into tears when he related that his squire might have to put down one of his carriages if the Corn Laws were repealed—if one could feel sure that that story was true.

Perhaps the most eloquent symbol of this attachment to one class and severance from another could be seen in the trouble about pews. Since the sixteenth century pews had come to be attached to certain houses or to be owned by private persons, they were bought and sold and even included in marriage settlements. Ownership was obtained by a faculty from the bishop's court or by prescription. Churches were renovated or built by the sale of rights in pews, the clergy were sometimes partly paid from pew rents, and, however obtained, a fierce sense of private property in pews was excited, as it was in the angry man who once after service complained to Archbishop Magee, in his early days as a curate, about a stranger who had intruded himself into the large pew of which he was the sole occupant. 'Sir', said he, 'I would not dare to disturb Divine Service to pull him out of my pew, but I took the slight liberty of sitting upon his hat.'[1] The result of this system was that every part of the church too often became appropriated to the well-to-do, and the poor were relegated to bare benches contemptuously placed in the most remote parts of the church, and were naturally apt to stay away. The system was the source of great evil and was much detested by the best clergy in the reforming times of the nineteenth century. But it was more than an abuse, it was a symbol of a Church too closely identified

[1] *Speeches and Addresses by the Late W. C. Magee, D.D.*, ed. Charles S. Magee, 1892, p. 208. Speech on the Parish Churches Bill; the whole speech is worth reading.

with property and social advantage, indeed with the social order of that old England of prescription, of privilege and of gross inequality.

In the Church of England, then, you have a body whose whole existence is so closely wrapped up with the history of the English race that it is impossible to say to what extent it has endowed that race with characteristics drawn from its nature, or assumed its own nature to comply with English characteristics. But its virtues have been the virtues of the English, and its vices their vices, or the vices of some of them. For some of its virtues perhaps a man could not do better than look into the Prayer Book, for some of its vices a cynic might say that the best thing might be also to look there, at the evasive language of some of the Thirty-nine Articles. But that would be unhistorical and unfair, and the worst of its vices you will not find so much in its Prayer Book as in its practice, where you will see evidence of its too close identification with certain classes of the state.

It is, however, only fair to remember that that identification was called for by the old theory of the social order. If it was true that authority and superintendence were rightly and naturally in the hands of the upper classes it was also right and natural that ecclesiastical authority should be associated with them in order to give it its due force. By such an association men of leisure and learning could give necessary guidance to those who could have the opportunity for neither. It is not our way of looking at things, but it is not wholly irrational. Yet as a social philosophy it was certain to cause trouble. The conditions of the sixteenth and seventeenth centuries were certain to cause religious disagreement, and that disagreement, bitter in any case, would be indefinitely embittered if religious differences were made to correspond with social and economic differences as well. It would add to the distaste of a man likely in any case to dissent from the practices of and the beliefs expounded in his parish church, if he was habitually treated by its parson as a social inferior. But that introduces the whole question of the relation of the Established Church to religious toleration, to which I turn in the next chapter.

VI

THE OLD ORDER AND
RELIGIOUS OPINION

'Every article therefore both of morals and religion may and ought to be tried in such manner as can be reasonably expected from the parts, attainments and circumstances of each person: and concerning this, we should judge modestly for ourselves, and consult others with deference.' Archbishop Secker (*Archbishop of Canterbury, 1758–68*): *Sermon on 1 Thess. v. 21, 22: 'Prove all things: hold fast to that which is good: abstain from all appearance of evil.'*

THE problem of religious toleration was clearly raised by the fact of the Church's establishment. A Church is supposed to be the living embodiment of certain opinions; if a Church is 'established' it would seem to mean that the opinions it embodies will be favoured by the state, and it may mean that those who disagree with those opinions will not enjoy the full privileges of the citizen, or even suffer actual persecution. Was then the maintenance of certain opinions part of the old order of English society and if that was so, how was that compatible with the boasted liberties of Englishmen, of which liberty of conscience was deemed to be one?

The question is important, and its answer is very complicated. There is no space here to go into the vexed history of religious toleration in England. Suffice it to say that the history of the seventeenth century had proved that the old idea of one Church for the whole nation was impossible in England, and that active persecution was, to put it at its lowest, politically impracticable; and, in a slightly higher range of values, probably wrong. After the Revolution that fact had been written into the Constitution by the so-called Toleration Act of 1689, which permitted freedom of worship to certain Dissenters under certain restricted conditions. An important lesson had been partially learnt, an important factor added to the English tradition.

But the lesson had after all only been partially learnt. Even the limited toleration which the Act of 1689 conceded was not secure; in the reign of Anne the Tories tried to go back on it, but the accession of George I frustrated their pious intentions. However, so fickle was the position that during the eighteenth century the Whig governments did not care to risk raising the cry 'The Church in Danger' by trying to repeal the Acts which imposed disabilities on Protestant Dissenters, and even in 1747, when the Carrs Lane Chapel in Birmingham was founded, it was considered wise to make provision for the disposal of the building should it become again illegal to employ it for the purpose of independent worship.[1] Moreover, what was conceded after the Revolution can truly be contemptuously described as toleration, not as religious equality, for bare toleration was all the Dissenters received. They could not enter fully into the public life of the country until the Test and Corporation Acts were repealed in 1828. In the eighteenth and the first half of the nineteenth centuries they could not matriculate at Oxford or take a degree at Cambridge. They had to pay a rate towards the upkeep of the Parish Church if the Churchwarden chose to levy one. After 1753, and possibly before, their marriages were not valid unless celebrated in the Parish Church, except in the case of Jewish and Quaker marriages, and when they died there was difficulty about the burial of a Dissenter in the Parish Churchyard.[2]

Such was the position of orthodox Protestant Dissenters, but the Toleration Act only extended to those who would subscribe to certain of the Thirty-Nine Articles, it did not extend to those who denied the Divinity of Christ, a fact which might have led to serious results in a century which saw the development of Deism and Unitarianism. The Roman Catholics still lay under the full weight of the Penal Laws, and if these were increasingly laxly administered, the fact that the fire of popular passion against Roman Catholics was only banked can be seen in the Gordon Riots in 1780, when much of London was burnt because attempts had been made to modify the laws against Papists.

But this intolerance was not confined to the mob; it was shared in the eighteenth and even in the nineteenth century by

[1] Dale, *The Life of R. W. Dale of Birmingham by his Son, A. W. Dale*, 1898, pp. 71 and 170.
[2] See W. G. Addison, *Religious Equality in Modern England*, London 1944. For Dissenters' marriages, see R. W. Dale, *History of English Congregationalism*, pp. 623 and 643.

men of education, while most of the divines of the eighteenth century seem in general to have been perfectly satisfied with what seems to us a completely indefensible situation. Part cause of this complacency was no doubt the blindness of conservatism. When Burke said in 1780, 'Toleration is a new virtue in any country. It is a late ripe fruit in the best climates',[1] he was thinking of the Gordon rioters, but the words have a much wider application. Yet if that conservatism was blind it was not unreasoned. Men not lacking in either conscience or ability were clear that the situation was theoretically justified. In fact they believed that the position of the Church of England, so far from diminishing the freedom of Englishmen, actually protected it. However, what they felt can best be understood from a quotation from a sermon preached by Bishop Butler before the House of Lords in 1747.

'Liberty', he says, 'which is the very genius of our civil constitution, and runs through every branch of it, extends its influence to the ecclesiastical part of it. A religious establishment without a toleration of such as think they cannot in conscience conform to it, is itself a general tyranny; because it claims absolute authority over conscience; and would soon beget particular kinds of the worst sort, tyranny over the mind, and various superstitions; after the way should be paved for them, as it soon must, by ignorance. On the other hand, a constitution of civil government without any religious establishment is a chimerical project of which there is no example: and which, leaving the generality without guide and instruction must leave religion to be sunk and forgotten amongst them; and at the same time give full scope to superstition, and the gloom of enthusiasm; which last, especially, ought surely to be diverted and checked, as far as it can be done without force. Now a reasonable establishment provides instruction for the ignorant, withdraws them, not in the way of force, but of guidance, from running after those kind of conceits. It doubtless has a tendency likewise to keep up a sense of real religion and real Christianity in a nation: and is moreover necessary for the encouragement of learning; some parts of which the scripture-revelation absolutely requires should be cultivated.'[2]

[1] *The Works of the Right Hon. Edmund Burke*, Edition of 1812, Vol. IX, p. 272, 'Thoughts on the approaching Executions.'
[2] Butler, *op. cit.*, Vol. 2, pp. 365–6.

This has been quoted at some length because it contains so much that has left its marks on the English tradition. The passage is important first because it is clear from its words that Butler fully accepts as did most leading English Churchmen in his day, toleration not as a mere political convenience but as an unquestioned principle. But what of the two conceits, superstition and enthusiasm, from which the Church was to withdraw men? They, too, are important because it was their nature which was believed to justify the inequalities of the law and the honoured position of the Church. Each was severally held to be embodied in the two groups of Christians who still lived under the shadow of the law, superstition in the Roman Catholic Church, enthusiasm among the Protestant Dissenters; and the errors of each were yearly celebrated with service and sermon on November 5th and January 30th respectively. What churchmen thought about each is worthy of consideration.

The hatred of Rome is one of the commonplaces of English history. It partly sprang, as cruel feelings often do spring, from fear, the fear of a forcible reconversion of the country by Roman Catholicism. That fear was grounded on the history of the sixteenth century, when it was not without its justification; but it survived long after that. It had been fed by the men who had manipulated the Popish Plot in the reign of Charles II, and given substance by the manœuvres of James II and the persecution of Protestants by Louis XIV. It survived even in the minds of reasonable people well into the eighteenth century, at least till after the Jacobite rebellion of 1745.[1] Both religious liberty and civil liberty were at stake, for the history of James II and the nature of Catholic Bourbon rule had encouraged the belief that there was a close correlation between Roman Catholicism and tyranny and 'arbitrary government', and men did not believe that the authority which the Roman Catholic Church claimed was compatible with the liberty that ought to be enjoyed by a Christian man.

There may or there may not be truth in that belief, but of course Englishmen were in no state of mind to judge it fairly as an abstract proposition. Centuries of prejudice, heated by fear, darkened by ignorance, fed, as in the irony of human affairs

[1] See Norman Sykes, *Edmund Gibson, Bishop of London, 1669–1748*, Oxford 1926, pp. 292–300.

cruel traditions so often are fed, by stories of martyrdom, had distorted English minds, the minds of Churchmen and Dissenters alike, on this subject; and the passion remained on well into the nineteenth century. Indeed, to illustrate its force it will be best to take words written in the middle of the century by one of the greatest English Churchmen of his day, a high Churchman who had a justified contempt for the vulgar Protestantism with which he had often come into conflict. Dean Hook in a letter to Mr. Gladstone in 1851 on the occasion of the assumption by the Roman Catholic bishops of territorial titles in this country, wrote as follows: 'I am boiling over with indignation at the attack which has been made upon the institutions of my country, my Church and my religion by an avowed wicked, and unscrupulous enemy. I believe that assailant to be the enemy of God and man, for although the Pope be the Antichrist employed against the cause of my Saviour and my God in this Country, the real author of the movement is he who is the author of all evil.'[1] If such an occasion could excite so good a man to use such wild words it may well be guessed how fierce was the long tradition that prompted them.

The objection to 'enthusiasm' and the Protestant Dissenters was also barbed by fear and irrelevant historical memories. But to understand this feeling it is necessary to understand the word 'enthusiasm', for much ignorant satire has been aimed against eighteenth-century Churchmen in the belief that the word had already shrunk to its modern meaning of 'gusto' or 'zeal'. The first definition of the word in Johnson's *Dictionary* is 'a vain belief in private revelation; a vain confidence of divine favour or communication'; and that meaning, except for the significant addition of the word 'vain', is, of course, justified by the word's derivation from the Greek. It was that 'vain belief' they feared. It was held that it was enthusiasm, an arrogant confidence that they were divinely inspired, that had led the sects to rise up and overturn Church and state in the seventeenth century, and cut off the king's head; it was held in particular that the tyrant Cromwell had been an interesting mixture of enthusiasm, ambition and cunning.[2] Therefore the lessons of the great Civil War were constantly and absurdly being cited against the Dissenters, until the French Revolution brought new fears, and also confirmed

[1] W. R. W. Stephens, *Life of Walter Farquhar Hook*, 1878, Vol. II, p. 295.
[2] Warburton, *op. cit.*, Book III, Sect. VI, Vol. 2, p. 280.

men's beliefs in the Dissenters' fundamental disloyalty.[1] The matter was continually rehearsed in the sermons preached on January 30th, the anniversary of the execution of Charles I, and the dangers of religious war were held to justify the civil disabilities of the Dissenters.[2]

So much for what was negative, and it is worth while to notice how much fear, ignorance, misapplied history have assisted in the make-up of human intolerance. But there was a positive side, and it was more respectable. To draw men from these conceits the Church of England did not claim to rely solely on its own authority nor yet solely on the authority of the Bible, it also claimed to appeal to reason and to scholarship, without which the Bible, as Butler pointed out somewhat obscurely, cannot rightly be interpreted. Without reason, indeed, the Bible may become simply the oracle for the vanity of the enthusiast, and the authority of the Church the potential vehicle of human tyranny. Indeed the appeal to human reason had come to be one of the main clauses in the case of the English Church, to be associated with the claims of antiquity and the pre-eminent authority of Scripture. Hooker had defended the rights of human reason against the Puritan claim that the Bible contained the answer to everything, and Chillingworth, another great Anglican apologist, had pointed out in controversy with a Jesuit that the human reason must be final authority over all authority. 'It being indeed a plain impossibility for any man to submit his reason but to Reason: for he that doth it to Authority must of necessity think himself to have greater reason to believe that Authority.'[3] Moreover, the plea that a man has the right to set aside the claim of authority can be found in the case made for freedom of speech and thought in Jeremy Taylor's *Liberty of Prophesying*.[4]

For the appeal to reason is a claim for human freedom. Reason is not simply the monopoly of divinely authorized Church or individual, reason cannot be forced, and if its rights are endorsed by God it is wrong to try. With the English Church the results of this consideration were unfortunately delayed by the circumstances of the time, by the fear of intolerant men forcing the issue

---

[1] Anthony Lincoln, *Some Political and Social Ideas of English Dissent*, Cambridge 1938, pp. 4–8.

[2] Warburton, *op. cit.*, Book II, Sect. VI, Vol. 2, p. 280 ff.

[3] Chillingworth, *Religion of Protestants* (London 1674), p. 74.

[4] Jeremy Taylor (London 1828), Vol. 8, p. 196.

citing as their authority the commands of God and their inter-
pretation of the Scripture, by Laud's sergeant-major mind,
and by the Church's entanglement with politics. But even
in the troubled times of the seventeenth century, some English
Churchmen had desired a more tolerant approach; Hales and the
Cambridge Platonists, as well as Chillingworth, pointed the way
to a world in which men should not be coerced into believing
speculative opinions, and when the time came and the political
game was played out the Church of England had been prepared
from within to accept toleration and reject persecution as a
tyranny 'of the worst sort, tyranny over the mind'.

That lesson came with all the greater force to the Churchmen of
the eighteenth century, when they looked back, as they often
did, at the ravages for which fanaticism had been responsible in
the century before. They were apt to believe that many of the
points in controversy between the Churches were doubtful, and
the duty of charity certain, and to reflect, to quote Bishop Butler
speaking on another, though cognate, topic, 'How far they can
with reason satisfy themselves in neglecting what is certainly
right on account of what is doubtful whether it be wrong'.[1] No
doubt they underestimated the importance of the points on which
their forefathers had lost their tempers, but possibly they had
learnt an important lesson. What it was can be best realized from
the fine words of Burke, in a speech whose general object was
indeed to protect, not to modify, the dogmatic standards of the
Church of England. 'I will not enter', he said, 'into the question
how much Truth is preferable to Peace. Perhaps Truth may be
far better. But as we have scarcely ever the same certainty in the
one, that we have in the other, I would, unless the Truth were
evident indeed, hold fast to Peace, which has in her company
Charity, the highest of the virtues'.[2]

Yet the appeal to reason and the appeal to charity are not the
same as the appeal to scepticism. The point is important because
it is sometimes asserted that it was only when men lost their faith
in revealed religion that they gave up persecution. These men,
however, were sincere Christians. Jeremy Taylor was a Christian,
Butler was a Christian, Burke was a Christian, even in Locke's
letters on Toleration you will find the expression of an apparent
belief in a minimum of Christianity. Toleration was not only

---

[1] Butler, *op. cit.*, Vol. II, p. 292.
[2] Burke, *op. cit.*, Vol. X, p. 15.

won by the steadfastness of Christians in a minority like the Congregationalists or the Quakers in the face of persecution, it was conceded by Christians in a majority because they were Christians, Christians who had learnt their lesson. Perhaps the course of history suggests that some element of doubt assists men to be tolerant. Certainly if you believe too much, if you believe that all the answers to all the problems are not only certain but self-evident, or clearly dictated by some divinely appointed authority, toleration to others who disagree may seem to be out of the question. But there is another side to the problem which is normally neglected. If you believe too little intellectual liberty may not be secure.

These men held sincerely to certain positive beliefs, the rights of the human intellect, the fact that charity is the 'highest of the virtues', and what they understood to be the lesson of the Gospels. If they had not believed in these things, there might have been less reason for them to have believed in toleration. It may be answered that there would also have been no reason for them to wish to be intolerant, but that, alas, is not true. If one reads the melancholy history of religious persecution it is difficult not to be struck by the extent to which fear, secular and political passions, social dislikes are mixed with the pure passion for truth. In England, indeed, these things seem to predominate; but history everywhere suggests that there are many other reasons for cruelty, even for the persecution of heretics, besides a belief in Christianity. In fact what seems to be generally needed is a reason for eschewing the convenience and gratification of cruelty, for no one will for long lack reason for indulging in it. However, the point was put with clarity in the late eighteenth century by Joseph Priestley, the great Unitarian divine. 'The doctrine of Toleration and religious liberty is now maintained on two very different and even opposite grounds. The one is an *indifference to all religion* and an opinion of the absolute insignificance of all distinctions of it; and the other its exceeding great *importance* to every man singly considered; so that everything relating to it is held sacred with him, and he cannot upon any consideration surrender his own right of determining concerning it, to any man or body of men upon earth.' And if we consider the history of the twentieth century, which has not been remarkable for its passionate belief in Christianity, or for its mercy, we may be tempted to conclude with him that 'These *unbelieving* statesmen have, therefore, within them the principles of the coolest and most unrelenting persecution'.[1]

What then the divines of the eighteenth-century Church claimed to fear was the return to power of the forces of superstition and enthusiasm which in their view had enslaved the human intellect, and provoked persecution and religious war. It was this that in large part the Established Church existed to prevent. For this its work of edification and guidance, its wealth and privileges were a necessity. The bishop must mix on equal terms with the noble, and the parochial clergy must not be dependent on their flocks for their sustenance as was the case with the dissenting minister, for it was important that the Church should be free to speak with independence and authority to everyone, from the highly placed and highly educated down to those 'whom Providence dooms to live on trust', because they had fewer opportunities for inquiry, or a less inquiring type of mind.[2]

That was the theory. Unhappily the facts fell some way short of it. It was unfortunate for the independence of the bishops that they were dependent on politicians for their appointment, it was trebly unfortunate that both bishops and clergy were so deeply committed to the prejudices and interests of the existing order of society. That, however, is not the worst count against them. On their own showing the most dangerous ally of superstition and enthusiasm was ignorance, and surely the proper answer to ignorance is not authoritative guidance but education? But the Church of England did not do enough for popular education. It is perfectly true that it did much more than is usually credited to it. Many of the grammar schools were founded by pious churchmen, they were often under the superintendence of the clergy, and the schoolmasters were often clergymen. In the eighteenth century the work of the S.P.C.K. and the Charity School and Sunday School movement were very important.[3] In the nineteenth century the effort was much greater.

[1] *Works of Joseph Priestley*, ed. J. T. Rutt, 1823, Vol. XXII, p. 270.

[2] *Works of Archdeacon Paley*, printed and published by J. F. Dove (no date), Vol. V, p. 256, Sermon III, 'A distinction of Orders in the Church depended on Principles of Public Utility'. Burke, *op. cit.*, Vol. V, pp. 176-200, *Reflections on the French Revolution*.

[3] M. G. Jones, *The Charity School Movement*, Cambridge University Press, 1938.

If one reads that lugubrious document, the Report of the Commission of Inquiry into the State of Public Education, which was produced in 1861, one is struck not only by the backwardness of the whole country, but also how considerable had been in very many cases the effort of the clergy of the Church of England and how heavy the burdens left upon their shoulders. They had given of their time, and they had given of their money so much that in some cases they had got themselves into financial difficulties.[1] To the provision of schools ought to be added the unseen results of directly parochial work. The catechetical instruction of children may have been neglected in far too many cases, but even such success as there was in fulfilling the old ideal of placing an educated gentleman in every village, had important effects in civilizing the wildness of the countryside. Indeed, evidence of this may perhaps be seen in the decline of the old belief in witchcraft, which had caused so much human misery in the past.

But the eighteenth-century record is not good enough, and probably the records of certain of the Swiss cantons, or of Scotland, show what might have been done if the ecclesiastical system had been different. Yet the whole issue raises one important problem which in due course will have to be considered. It can be raised by asking this question: given all the conditions, would it have really been possible to educate Hanoverian England so that every man could judge justly for himself the important questions that decide man's destiny? But the matter can be pressed further, it can be asked whether, with all our state-financed education, even now we provide adequate equipment for such a purpose to every man and woman, and pressed further still to ask whether where such equipment is provided, many men and women have the pertinacity or interest to apply it, as they should do if they wish to make up their own minds. In the old social order the answer was easy. Ignorant men were expected to look up to their betters for guidance, a position which can be partially defended by these words of Bishop Berkeley. 'I will freely own', says he, 'a judicial and impartial search after truth is the most valuable employment of the mind. Those who have the talents and will be at the pains cannot do better than engage in that noble pursuit. But those who are not qualified by age or education; those who have neither disposition, nor leisure, nor faculties to dig in the mine of truth

[1] 1861, Command Paper XXI, pp. 77–8. See also Frank Smith, *The Life and Work of Sir James Kay-Shuttleworth*, London 1923.

themselves, must take what is retailed out by others. I see no remedy.'[1] The important question may be whether, thinking honestly over the modern situation, we see any remedy either.

But to raise this question is to look rather far ahead. To turn back to the old order, it must be confessed that the Hanoverian Church viewed its position with profound self satisfaction. Even the active and the intelligent were not inclined to see anything wrong with the situation. Churchmen were proud of the Church, proud of its reasonableness, proud of its wealth, proud of its learning. Above all, it was the Established Church, and for a nation to have no religious establishment was 'a chimerical project of which there is no example'. Dissenters were looked upon with contempt, the Church was the nation, the Dissenters overscrupulous eccentrics from the lower or middling classes. The general attitude can be perhaps not unfairly summed up by some words of a sermon preached in defence of the Church of England before the University of Cambridge, in 1838, six full years after the Reform Bill. 'We are justified, I trust', said the preacher, 'in treating of the collective nation as a Christian community and considering the general sense of that community as expressed by the sentiments which are held within the pale of our ecclesiastical system. For without overlooking the fatal differences of opinion, especially on doctrinal points, beyond our limits, we cannot but feel how much influence the higher education and higher social standing of the individuals of our communion have upon those who formally dissent from it, and how nearly the intellectual and moral judgements of the nation at large are represented by our own.'[2]

Already by the time these confident words were spoken, nemesis was at the door, if not in the house. Some fifty years before this sermon was preached the French Revolution had started, and it might be said that even then the old order of things had been summoned before the judgement seat of history, and had been condemned. Men were no longer prepared to accept the prescriptive rights of princes or nobles, or of anyone, as part

[1] Berkeley, op. cit., Vol. II, p. 231. From 'A discourse addressed to Magistrates'.

[2] Merivale, The Church of England a faithful witness of Christ not destroying the law, but fulfilling it. Four Sermons preached before the University of Cambridge in November, 1838, by the Rev. Charles Merivale, H. M. Fellow of St. John's College, Pitt Press, 1839.

of the natural order of the universe. In due course, it was held, they would disappear; the problem was whether the Church would follow them wherever she had too intimately associated her lot with the old order of things. Or indeed the matter might go further, it seemed possible that Christianity itself might disappear also.

For one of the great movements that had germinated in the eighteenth century had been the development of disbelief in Christianity. Leaving the Jews out of account, the English Deists of the eighteenth century were probably the first men in these islands since the conversion of the Danes openly to reject Christianity, and yet live. The strain on the newly discovered principle of toleration was very great and shows itself in the letters of prelates at the time. Indeed the roughness with which clerical controversialists treated their opponents suggests that they might easily have turned to rougher methods still. Fortunately they were not able to do so, partly it must be confessed because of the caution and indifference of the government, and a nobler answer to the Deists was found in Bishop Butler's *Analogy*. Yet though in that intellectual battle the Church held her own, it was never again to be the case that England was a country in which every man was professedly Christian.

On the Continent the matter went further and in due course those who attacked Christianity joined forces with those who attacked the powers of kings and of aristocrats, and in many countries the great issue seemed to be between the Roman Catholic Church and the godless revolution. It is a very important fact that it was not so in England. No doubt this was partly because in England no political revolution was necessary and also because so many Englishmen had been influenced by the great Evangelical revival. But it was partly a result of that great lesson of respect for reason which the English Church had learnt and taught. It was because the Deists had been met with argument that they had met more effectual intellectual resistance in England than on the Continent. It was because in England persecution had not been pressed as far and maintained as long, as had been the case in some Roman Catholic countries, that other Christian sects survived in strength outside the official Church, and these could be made the effective vehicle of the new forces that were to control the nineteenth century.

The Protestant Dissenters, who were to play a great part in

the new century, were sober folk not likely to be led astray into
the vagaries of revolution or to be attracted by the godless or
deistical Jacobin of the Continental revolution, and they were
hard-working folk, more like to make money than speeches, or
rather in many cases likely to make money as well as speeches;
for at no period have the English Dissenters been exactly inarticulate. But as the new century went forward their power was
to increase till they became what they had not been since the
seventeenth century, a really important factor in the political life
of the country. Therefore in England the conflict between old
and new was not in the nineteenth century to be between a
Christian Church and opponents who listed Christianity as one
of the things which had most noticeably enslaved the spirit of
men, but between two groups of Christians, the Church of
England, largely, but by no means uniformly, conservative, and
English Dissent, with the temporary exception of the Wesleyans,
clmost uniformly Liberal and Radical. It is probable that that
aommon Christianity has led to a fundamental national unity,
an ultimate agreement on essentials, which has had most important results in the history of England.

So much for the good the old ecclesiastical order bequeathed
to English history. Its failures also left their mark. There was a
bitter price to pay for past pride and self-satisfaction. The disabilities which the law imposed on the Dissenters remained into
the nineteenth century, and well on into the nineteenth century,
sometimes into the third quarter of that century. As securities for
the Church of England they were worthless, but to the Dissenters
they were naturally intolerable badges of inequality. As their
power increased they turned with wrath on the Church of
England, aiming at that Church's disendowment and disestablishment, and the bitterness of that assault and the dangers which the
Church had to face had been deserved by its failure to do justice
in the time of its strength.

Even the virtues on which the Established Church had prided
itself had not been as valuable to Church and nation as might
have been expected from the laudatory accounts which the
eulogists had given. The belief in scholarship was justifiable, since
scholarship is necessary to discipline the beliefs which man
adapts as his guide. It is a storehouse of reason which man
neglects to his peril. Yet though there had been considerable
learning in the eighteenth-century Church of England, from

which the nation drew greater advantages than is usually assumed, yet it would be idle to pretend that the Church's pre-eminence in learning fully justified the advantages it itself enjoyed. Oxford and Cambridge, the preserves of the Church, were in the eighteenth century allowed to slip into gross indolence and corruption, while much of the learning which did exist was in linguistic classical scholarship and by itself of no great value in assisting man to solve the great problems proposed to him. In fact it is probable that the best advanced general education in eighteenth-century England was to be obtained in the academies which the Dissenters organized.

With the claim to present a learned and reasonable Christianity to the nation, had been associated the claim to control the dangers of superstition and enthusiasm. Now the fear of both these things is justified; if they are properly defined they are alike dangerous to truth, man's freedom, and true religion. But they are difficult to define, and eighteenth-century churchmen were far too perfunctory in their methods of definition and therefore too little just in their results. Much that they condemned as superstitions were in reality practices and beliefs by means of which men were really finding their way to the Mercy Seat; and if Englishmen had been able to understand that fact they might have been more nearly just to the Roman Catholics, and perhaps avoided nemesis in Ireland. The same considerations apply to the condemnation of enthusiasm. If enthusiasm is really a 'vain belief' in divine inspiration it must be condemned; the devastation to morals, to social order, to a man's own religion which such a belief may cause is writ large in history. It is possible, too, that the dangers of enthusiasm are particularly great for ignorant people, and people without strong traditions, for it must always be remembered that ignorance and low estate have their own forms of intolerable arrogance. But what if the belief is not entirely vain? What if the Holy Spirit is at work, as often in history, among the lowly and the ignorant in reproof of what has grown cold and formal and purse proud? It is very easy to make mistakes in this matter. The judges of Joan of Arc made a mistake in the fifteenth century, and one might say with reverence that a yet more hideous mistake was made by certain rulers and pharisees and priests fourteen centuries before. Indeed so many and so terrible are the mistakes which intellectual and ecclesiastical leaders have made from time to time that one must often turn uneasily from the pride of scholarship, from what is authorized and commended by the order of society, be it aristocratic or communist, to wonder what, or who, is being brought to birth in the dwelling places of the ignorant and of the people of little account.

The condemnation of enthusiasm not only encouraged Churchmen to continue to be unjust to Dissenters, it was also part cause of the Church's worst mistake in a matter that touched the most serious peril of all. Speaking of Whitefield, Bishop Butler had said to John Wesley, 'Sir, the pretending to extraordinary revelations and gifts of the Holy Ghost is a horrid thing, a very horrid thing'.[1] Wesley denied that he himself made any such claim, but claimed as a priest the duty to preach the Gospel where there was need. The results of the conflict which that conversation suggests are well known, they are writ large in the loss of the Wesleyans. The leaders of the Church should not be condemned out of hand. In the hands of Wesley and Whitefield the evangelical revival could not and would not respect the discipline of the existing parochial and diocesan organization of the Church, and it is hard to condemn the prelates of the Church for wishing to protect that organization. When the evangelical revival was prepared to accept that parochial organization, it found its place in the Church of England with very important results for that Church and for the nation.[2] Yet for all this it would be hard to deny that the rigidity, inadequacy and self-sufficiency of the Church of England is condemned by the Wesleyan schism; and perhaps the most serious article in the accusation is the fact that many of those to whom the Wesleyans went would probably otherwise have hardly heard of Christianity at all.

Therein at the turn of the century lay not only the worst failure of the Church but the most deadly danger. The parochial system of the Church did not and could not minister to all the people of England. It was not only a question of clerical indifference or indolence or non-residence where that was to be found, it was not a question only of the outcasts, the felons, the rabble, or the miners, or the sailors, but of areas where the parochial system did not work through sheer physical incapacity, of towns which had grown beyond the capacity of their parishes, of

[1] *Butler's Works, op. cit.*, Vol. II, p. 435; quoted from Vol. XIII of the *Works of John Wesley*, Edition of 1872.

[2] C. H. Smyth, *Simeon and Church Order*, Cambridge 1940.

country places which had always been much too large for the
incumbent who was supposed to minister to them, or where two
or more livings had had to be joined because of the poorness of
the benefices. It would be interesting to know how much sheer
savagery and brutal ignorance had always lurked in the dark
places of England. But in the late eighteenth century and in the
nineteenth, these dark spots were growing. The population was
increasing, and increasing enormously, far beyond the numbers
eighteenth-century institutions could minister to, or even govern.

It is that fact that more than anything else created the menace
and misery of the first half of the nineteenth century. The new
industrialism may have increased though it did not create the
evils of child labour, the new commerce may have forced too
many people to live at the mercy of a fluctuating market, the new
politics may have threatened bloody revolution. But the worst
horror and true danger of the situation came from the new masses
gathered together in vast urban conglomerations for whom no
proper sanitation could have been provided, for whom no
reasonable houses existed, for whom there was in most cases
no proper town government, and for whom above all there
was no spiritual provision whatsoever.

As the century developed men became conscious of the situation; in the dark year of 1840, in No. CXXXIV of the *Quarterly
Review* there appeared an article, which, as was natural in a Tory
periodical at that moment, portrayed the situation in sombre
colours. But it also proposed a remedy which was compatible
with, no, grew out of, the old conception of a society ordered
by law and inspired by the Church. Its last passage was as follows:
'But here comes the worst of all—those vast multitudes, ignorant
and excitable in themselves, and rendered still more so by
oppression or neglect, are surrendered, almost without a struggle,
to the experimental philosophy of infidels and democrats. When
called upon to suggest our remedy of the evil, we reply by an
exhibition of the cause of it; the very statement involves an
argument, and contains its own answer within itself. Let your
laws, we say to the Parliament, assume the proper functions of
law, protect those for whom neither wealth, nor station, nor age
have raised a bulwark against tyranny; but above all, open your
treasury, erect Churches, send forth the ministers of religion,
reverse the conduct of the enemy of mankind, and sow wheat
amongst the tares—all hopes are groundless, all legislation weak,

all conservatism nonsense without this Alpha and Omega of policy; it will give content instead of bitterness, engraft obedience on religion, raise purity from corruption, and life from the dead.'[1]

The writer of the article was Lord Ashley, afterwards the seventh Earl of Shaftesbury,[2] and in that critical period, when a new world was struggling into existence with new hopes and new possibilities, but with slums for its dwelling places and slavery for its children, no man did more than Shaftesbury to make law 'assume the proper functions of law', to protect those who could not protect themselves. That was the object of the Ten Hours Bill for which he had to fight so hard, of his other measures to protect women and children in industry, that was the object of his hard and unrewarding work for public health. Throughout his long life, always uneasy, often oversensitive, but ever obedient to his Master, he worked unceasingly to recover those whom society had so ruthlessly surrendered, and the value of his service could hardly be exaggerated.

But Shaftesbury was, of course, exceptional. Others of his class and of his politics did not reach his high standard, and in his own county of Dorset and on his own father's estate he found to his great bitterness how notably the aristocratic principle had failed to protect and to foster those who should have been its first charge. Nor could he get his party to adopt the policy which he desired, without which, as he said, 'all conservatism' was 'nonsense'. For various reasons his leaders failed him, but this was not due to their coldness of heart. It was because times had changed, and the opportunities, if they had existed, had been lost. In 1818 it had still been possible to open the treasury to build churches for the Church of England. Many had believed that the Conservative Party should in Sir Robert Peel's great ministry of 1841–6 set its hand to this work, but it is quite clear that it had already become impossible to use public money for such a purpose. The world had changed since 1818. The forces of religious dissent had already become too strong and too belligerent for Church and state to work in equal partnership to meet the problems which the century was to produce.

As always in England the change was not to be complete, nor

[1] *Quarterly Review*, No. CXXXIV, Article V.
[2] Edwin Hodder, *The Life and Work of the Seventh Earl of Shaftesbury*, 1886. Vol. I, pp. 322 *ff.*

the resultant position logical. The Church was not in the nineteenth century to be disestablished, though earnest efforts were to be made to secure that end, but it was rightly to lose many of its special privileges, and above all it could never have such financial assistance from the government as would enable it to do the work of education and reclamation which Shaftesbury had seen to be necessary. That work, if done, was to be increasingly done by the secular state.

Yet in England the forces which brought this about, which first imposed the lesson of freedom and then the need for state organization, were themselves largely organized by Christian bodies. They too have left deep marks on the English inheritance, therefore to those forces we must now turn.

VII

RELIGION AND LIBERTY—
PURITANS AND REFORMERS

'We must be free or die, who speak the tongue
That Shakespeare spake; the faith and morals hold
Which Milton held.'

Wordsworth: Poems Dedicated to National Independence
and Liberty, XVI.

SO far I have dealt with what might be called the traditional, the conforming, factors in the English heritage, the law, the hierarchy of society, the Established Church and 'the Constitution in Church and state under which', as Shaftesbury confided to his diary in 1840, 'the mercy of God has hitherto appointed us to live';[1] and I have tried to show that whatever else they were, they were at least mixed with Christian conceptions. The law was held to guarantee those rights which the Creator of the universe had conferred on those who inhabited it, the Church was to teach and to administer the religion of Christ, even the traditional order of society prescribed for all men duties which they must perform, remembering 'the strict and solemn account which they must at one time make'. Indeed, all these things were in conception attempts to compass the difficult task of applying the doctrines of Christianity to the recalcitrant material of human society. Of course as attempts to apply anything that could remotely be called Christianity by anyone to anything at all it may be agreed that they were often egregious failures. The law could be savage and perverse, the Church ill organized and torpid, and the order of society more apt to confer privileges and to condone inequality than to exact duty. But it is good to keep in mind the fact that to reasonable humane and devout men these very imperfect things were believed to embody the principles of Christianity. It is good to keep this in mind partly because it is healthy to remember that every attempt to

[1] *Op. cit.*, Vol. I, p. 288.

embody the principles of Christianity in its institutions by any human community is certain to fail, but not likely to fail uselessly; and partly because the Nonconformists, the men who were to reject something of that traditional order, were also to claim that they revolted in the name of Christianity. The conflict was to be that of two Christian traditions, mixed of course with the dross of much that had little to do with Christianity.

It was also a conflict within one national tradition; in any age there have been few things more English than an English Church parson, unless it be an English Nonconformist. In each case, as was inevitable, much had been utilized to create the tradition that was of foreign inspiration, but in each case the tradition had been developed in an English context, coloured by English animosities, worked out in English traditions and moulded by, and helping to mould, the English temperament; and each side claimed to be defending that freedom which was supposed to a peculiar degree to be the Englishman's 'birthright'.

Yet the history of Nonconformity and of Puritanism may suggest a profounder conception of the relation of freedom to Christianity than is likely to be gained from that old conception of freedom as an Englishman's birthright. Presumably a birthright is earned by the simple, and reasonably undiscriminating, process of being born, an inheritance is gained by the testator dying and the heir coming into his own, without consideration of the nature and capacities of the heir. It is true that there may be a struggle to secure or maintain the inheritance. As Curran said in Dublin in 1790, 'The condition upon which God hath given liberty to man is eternal vigilance', and our forefathers in England were often invigorated by the reflection that 'the best period of the Constitution' was at some point in the past, and that in their own unhappy and degenerate times it was daily violated and menaced by new and peculiarly insidious enemies. But refreshing and salutory as such reflections were, they did not suffice to lead men from the consideration of the machinery which seemed necessary to secure freedom to the much deeper problem of what a man must be or be able to become, if he is rightly to be called free.

The tendency was, and indeed often is, to equate the idea of freedom with the idea of a man being at liberty to do what he wants with as little interference from outside as is compatible with the freedom of others; a healthy, useful and simple conception of which the profounder political thinkers are sometimes too apt to lose sight. But the history of freedom may suggest that even this elementary conception may not be realized unless what a man wants to do has an importance which will embolden him to outface the pressures which the state or society or brute circumstances may impose upon him. And if one advances the conception by a very little, if one goes on to the idea that the free man is the man who can fulfil himself freely, then surely he must develop a self to fulfil, and if so to be free will not only mean that there is an inheritance to be enjoyed, it may also mean that there is a life to be lived.

Now, if this is true, and it will be best to develop the theme rather by example than argument, it will clearly alter the conception of the relationship between Christianity and freedom. Probably the simplest conception of that relationship is that the enjoyment of freedom is a right with which the Creator of the universe has endowed each of His creatures, the right not to be simply the tool or chattel of others. That by itself is indeed an important principle, which men find it very difficult to respect. It cost the eighteenth and early nineteenth centuries a terrific struggle to honour it in the person of the negro slave, and perhaps they never fully learnt to honour it in the persons of their own poor. But by itself it is a passive conception, still suggesting a gift once given and thereafter enjoyed, and not a state to be achieved with difficulty by the free man. If that idea is true, then the connexion between religion and freedom will be more intimate.

But, if so, it is an intimacy that the eighteenth-century thinkers were not likely to understand, for there seems to have been a certain tendency then to conceive that the most important problem to which the relation between freedom and religion gave rise was not the problem in what way religion guaranteed freedom, but how best freedom could be guaranteed against religion, or perhaps they would say, against the excesses practised in the name of religion. This was a not unnatural view in a generation which looked back on the persecutions and civil wars of the sixteenth and seventeenth centuries with disgust, and was at the back of all the talk about superstition and enthusiasm. With some reason they felt they had come to civility and peace out of great tribulation, which was indeed once and for all guaranteed by the glorious revolution of 1688. 'It was at our great political revolution', said a preacher in 1838, 'that for the first time, presumably in human history, the prerogatives of secular society and the claims of Christianity were 'placed on an intelligible and practical footing'.[1]

But, as was not seldom the case, the situation was not so simple nor their own solution as final as the men of the eighteenth-century tradition conceived, and to understand the matter it is necessary to turn back to those conscience-tormented centuries which had passed before that happy balance was secured. In particular it is important to turn to two great historic processes which helped to provide the argument for their tragedy. One is what is called the creation of the modern state, and the other that great religious earthquake which caused the two rival movements of Reformation and Counter-Reformation.[2]

There is no time to describe either of these more than per-functorily, but in the sphere of the state, speaking very roughly, what happened was this: in the later middle ages the institutions of Europe in many cases lost vitality and effectiveness, and in various countries there was a breakdown in the order of the state and as a result civil war, such as our own Wars of the Roses. Where this had happened order was restored by the kings; rulers like Louis XI in France, our own Henry VII and VIII, or Ferdinand and Isabella in Spain. The work was welcome to most people, except those who had a direct interest in chaos or pillage, and the new monarchy formed a nucleus round which could form the gradually developing sense of nationality in the great nations of Europe. But all this meant a gradual change in men's conception of the rights of government. In the old days it had been possible for the ancient and inherent rights of certain individuals and some corporations, particularly of the greatest corporation of all, the clergy, to be urged, or even vindicated, against the secular ruler. But it was behind ancient privilege that the forces of disorder had lurked: if there was to be order in the state the forces of privilege, particularly hereditary privilege, must be bridled by some overriding will representing the community. Therefore the current in human affairs set towards the modern theory of the sovereign state, of which I have spoken in an earlier chapter, the theory by which all law derived from the will of the supreme power in the state against which no man, or body of men, could, at least in strict law, have any rights at all.

[1] Sermon by the Rev. Charles Merivale, already quoted.
[2] For the political thought of the sixteenth century, see J. W. Allen, *A History of Political Thought in the Sixteenth Century*, London 1928.

This development forms the matter of a very complicated and lengthy portion of European history. If one phase of it started in the fifteenth century, it was not completed in the sixteenth century and it is still important in the seventeenth. It was probably a development necessary to secure good government and to master forces which might otherwise have torn society to pieces in their greed and ferocity. It was also necessary for the ultimate development of democracy. But in all its phases it was dangerous to human freedom, and it was particularly so in the sixteenth and seventeenth centuries since in those centuries the will of the state that was likely to prevail at law was not the will of the people but the will of the monarch, reigning absolutely. Wherever the road led in the end, in the seventeenth century it seemed to lead logically through the courts of Versailles.

And then there was the great religious upheaval. What power it was that commanded the dry bones to live or through what agencies it operated is beyond the compass of this book to enquire. Suffice it to say that in the sixteenth century there was a tremendous movement of the spirit in man. It took different shapes, and surged in different directions, according to the time or place at which it appeared, or the traditions under which it operated, or whether it was summoned by Martin Luther, or such men as Ignatius Loyola, but it left no European country unchanged, few without profound divisions, and few human beings except the extremely illiterate or the unusually indifferent unaffected and quiet. In many cases its result was war. It has been said that every truth-seeker comes to bring not peace on earth but a sword, and very certainly that was true of the sixteenth century. In that century the detestable tradition of religious persecution was almost everywhere accepted, and acted upon; therefore a religious minority was normally faced with the ugly dilemma that either they must be content for His sake to be killed like sheep all day long or they must take the sword to save the remnants of Christ's flock alive. And if they won their battle they too were likely to feel it to be their duty to eliminate their opponents.

Now these terrible proceedings could not be without their effect on the other historic process, the development of the power of the state and of the monarch, and in some ways they helped that development. For one thing Protestant rulers had repudiated the power of Rome which had in the past, and had

G

still in theory, the right to curb kings and rulers and nations, so that after the Reformation even in theory Protestant rulers could be sovereign in a sense that they could not have been before. It is probable that in practice this made but little difference, for of recent years the power of the papacy had been but a ghost of what it once had been, and sixteenth-century kings, however Catholic, were not easily curbed. What is more important is the fact that here was more disorder to make those who loved peace cling more anxiously to the throne, and not only those who loved peace. In these ghastly struggles it was necessary for a dominant religious party to lean heavily, if it could, on the secular ruler of the land and, while promoting its own views, to enhance his authority and serve his purposes, be he Protestant godly prince or favoured son of the Church, Tudor, Stewart or Habsburg.

But in a profounder and more significant way the religious upheaval presented the most effective challenge, almost the only effective challenge, to the new sovereign state. A religious party in opposition, and under persecution, naturally joined forces with any other elements that were threatened or incommoded by the power of the king, be they factious nobles, discontented provinces, or rising economic class. To such oppositions the new religious element gave a courage, a fixity of purpose, and an organization which otherwise they would have lacked. More, it gave them a theory. To oppose the king it was necessary to question the power of kings. That had been done before, the ideas were there to be fitted to the new situation, but it was no light task in that king-ridden century to give them utterance. Yet where the king was a persecutor, or an idolator or a heretic, it was necessary to question his power in the name of the law of God, or the right of the Church, or even the will of the people: thus both Calvinist and Jesuit were responsible for important developments in the theory of politics. But the matter went deeper still. The religious movements of the sixteenth and seventeenth centuries produced persecutors enough, but they also produced martyrs; and every martyr, Catholic or Protestant, was in one way a witness to the same cause. No doubt they profoundly disagreed, no doubt many of them would have killed or tormented one another if they had had the chance, no doubt their successors repudiate one another, but every martyr testifies to the fact that there are some points on which a man may not obey any secular authority, and that some men will stand firm on those points however terrible the penalty. While that is true, freedom exists, whatever tyrannies prevail. But clearly the matter in which the martyr exercises his freedom must be something which he deems to be important enough for him to sacrifice everything else for its sake, it must be enforced by a sanction which transcends the sanctions which ordinarily control human beings. For if such freedom is the gift of the Creator to His creatures, it must also, even if that is a paradox, be bought by them for a price.

Nor is there any assurance that the price paid will purchase freedom for others than the martyr himself, for history does not seem to confirm the comfortable assumption that persecution will in no case be successful in accomplishing the work it sets out to do. Yet for all that the martyrs and the religious enthusiasts of the sixteenth and seventeenth centuries did produce lasting and practical achievements which are very important in the history of the freedom of man. In the sixteenth century the most important of these was probably the successful revolt of the Netherlands, but it seems likely that in the next century the most important events in the successful development of human freedom took place in England, for the English revolution was of critical significance not only for herself but for the world.

In neither case was the struggle wholly religious. In both the Low Countries and in England secular and religious motives and factors are inextricably woven or tangled together. Indeed the form which the struggle took in England was dictated in part by an event which has a much closer connexion with the development of the modern secular sovereign state than with any religious revival. Henry VIII's Reformation was, strictly speaking, not a religious reformation at all. It was the insolent triumph of the secular state over an ancient institution, the universal Church, which in one particular had not been subservient enough to the will of the king. Its object was the consolidation of power, not the purity of religion; the abuses of the ecclesiastical organization were left untouched and the king piously burnt Protestants while at the same time he hanged or beheaded those Roman Catholics who were courageous enough to refuse the oath of supremacy.

However, the great religious forces that were dividing the world could not be left out of England, neither by the waters of the North Sea and the Channel, nor certainly by the masterful will of a mortal king; and to whatever forces that were to dominate England, or to seek to dominate England, the king had dictated what weapons were to be used. He had set up a royal supremacy over the Church, but his chosen instrument for doing this was parliament, and in particular the House of Commons whose growth he fostered for his own purposes. Thereafter each religious settlement, Edward's, Elizabeth's, or even Mary's, was initiated by parliamentary authority, and, more than that, those who wished to change or develop a religious settlement, particularly the Puritans who wished to purify Elizabeth's religious settlement according to the revealed word of God, as interpreted by Calvin, were encouraged by this precedent to look to the House of Commons as the agent by means of which they could bring about a godly reformation in the face of the bewildering recalcitrance of their dear mistress the Queen.

Moreover another point in the history of those Elizabethan Puritans helped to place a secular institution, the House of Commons, rather strangely in the centre of the English religious controversy. The natural weapon of the Protestant Reformation in the late sixteenth century was the organization of a Presbyterian Church after the model of Geneva, indeed it was the effectiveness of this organization which helped to give Calvinism its great fighting power. It could be built up secretly cell by cell in the face of a hostile government, it could be made to accommodate itself to the natural habits of the most diverse political allies, and in Elizabeth's reign men attempted to build up such an organization within the Church of England. But they failed. The authorities of the English Church, Whitgift, Archbishop of Canterbury, and Bancroft, Bishop of London, were too much for them. The organization was broken up and the clerical leaders of the party dragged before the Courts of High Commission and Star Chamber. Nevertheless one platform lay open and remained open for the Puritans. It was Parliament and the House of Commons.

The sequel is obvious. The force and vigour of English Puritanism in the early seventeenth century became enlisted, not to press the claim of a reformed Church assembly to reform the religion of the country, but to secure that this should be done by a secular institution, parliament, which should displace the royal supremacy. The Puritans were well represented among those classes that supplied the most important members of the Commons. They found allies there; lawyers, country gentlemen, men engaged in commerce, who for diverse causes in the last years of Elizabeth and under the first two Stuarts found increasingly cogent secular reasons for wishing to oppose the king. So the Puritan cause became merged in the parliamentary side of the great struggle between king and parliament.

The great civil war in England was in its way a struggle between two religious systems struggling for mastery, more merciful indeed, but in origin not entirely unlike the religious wars in France, the Low Countries, and Germany; but it was also a constitutional struggle between king and parliament. It has been said by an eminent historian that but for the religious issue the civil war would never have broken out: no very deep study of its course is needed to establish the fact that but for Puritanism parliament would never have won. But the final result was wholly constitutional, the fruits of victory were gathered by parliament but not by Puritanism. The religious movement had performed in England an all important service for freedom. It had been, with the law, one of the main agents in preventing the establishment here of an absolute monarchy. It had saved others, but for itself in the settlement after 1660 it could not even secure toleration.

And if that was all there would be little to be said here about Puritanism. Certainly the part played in the history of English freedom by Puritanism would still have been important but it would not probably have been necessary to consider Puritanism as part of the living English heritage. It would be an important historical factor, and an interesting memory, but not something that could be considered to be inherited by modern England. The Restoration Parliament which was the immediate inheritor of the position gained by the Long Parliament was anything but Puritan in tone, in fact if there was one thing that the majority of them in it hated and feared it was a Puritan, for many of them had suffered under the Puritans during the Commonwealth. Even when the political pendulum swung back it never in the seventeenth century swung back in the direction of the Puritans. They remained a minority, before the revolution of 1688 a persecuted minority, after 1688 a tolerated minority in an uncongenial world.

But, leaving the accidents of history out of account, it would seem that the religious opinions of the majority of the Long Parliament were not likely to make a permanent contribution to the history of English freedom. Many members opposed the king for secular reasons, and found the Puritans useful allies. Others had religious reasons of a sort for their opposition, but they were vague and ephemeral, such reasons as a dislike of Laud and the High Church clergy, a dislike of bishops who meddled in politics or with men's private lives or private interests, or a fear that Laud and even the king were playing hand in glove with popery. Where there were more definite religious opinions in that parliament they were usually Presbyterian, and if the parliamentarians had achieved their ends they would have fastened on the country the rigidly disciplined Presbyterian system rather as it existed in Scotland, only with parliament rather than the Church controlling the whole, an arrangement which any Scot knew not to be the real thing. It is unlikely that it would have lasted, for Presbyterianism never seems to have struck deep roots in England except in a very few districts. And it would not have made for freedom. For the Presbyterians of that date were less intellectually tolerant than their High Church opponents.

Moreover even in secular matters that parliament's enthusiasm for freedom was inclined to stop short with the freedom of parliament. The remnant of parliament, even when the moment of its election was remote by eight or nine years of acute national division and civil war, in which many members of parliament had fought for the king, in its own view still spoke without question for the people of England. They held that if their voice was predominant in the state, then all was well: there was no need to think further. But all was not well. What parliament proposed at the end of the first civil war would probably have created a government as irresponsible as that of any Stuart king, and probably more powerful; and there were those who saw very clearly the need to think further, men who were not to be overlooked because they included most of the leaders and of the rank and file of that army which had enabled parliament to win the war. To emphasize matters parliament was prepared to treat their troops with base ingratitude. They would not give them the full pay that was owing to them; they would not provide adequate legal protection for such illegalities as they were bound to have committed during a civil war; it was inherently probable that once they were disbanded parliament would start to persecute many of the soldiers since many of them were members of sects such as the Independents or Baptists who rejected the Presbyterian system. The answer of the army was therefore to question parliament's title deeds and, after futile negotiations with parliament and the captive king and a second civil war, to take order in 1648 and 1649 with both, to purge parliament and cut off the king's head and to rule the country through one type of constitution or another till the death of their great leader Oliver Cromwell.

Now the rule of Cromwell and his associates was the rule of a minority whose sole title to power lay in the possession of the sword. It began with what most Englishmen believed to be a detestable crime, nor was it able in its course to conciliate the opinion of the majority of the nation. It failed to establish a satisfactory parliamentary system, neither Cavalier, nor Presbyterian, nor even extreme Leveller came to love it. Moreover the rule was often harsh, often over-puritanical and always expensive. When Oliver died and his military force was dissipated the nation returned with joy to the king and the ancient ways. The restored parliament set about persecuting the Puritans lest these things should ever happen again; and as we have seen men remembered what had happened with fear and detestation for more than a century afterwards. Yet paradoxically the examples and beliefs of these men are of immense significance in the living tradition of English freedom, and that is partly because, even more paradoxically, among those beliefs was a sincere, and a very deep-rooted, love for freedom.

You can see that passion for freedom in the man of genius who became Latin Secretary to the Council of State in 1649. There was much that was odious in Milton. His controversial violence was outrageous, his egoism great, yet there can be little question about his passion for freedom. His greatest poem *Paradise Lost* is the drama of men and angels created free even to disobey. Of the angels Milton causes Gabriel to tell Adam:

> *Freely we serve*
> *Because we freely love, as in our will*
> *To love or not: in this we stand or fall:*
> *And some are fallen, to disobedience fallen.*
> *And so from Heaven to deepest Hell; O fall*
> *From what high state of bliss, into what woe!*[1]

And of man, Milton tells us in its earliest line that the poem is 'Of man's first disobedience'. Disobedience foreseen by Omnipotence

[1] Book V, l. 538.

but not prevented, and redeemed not by power but by the incarnation and suffering of the Son of God.

> So Man as is most just
> Shall satisfy for Man, be judged and die,
> And dying rise, and rising with him raise
> His brethren, ransomed with his own dear life.[1]

It is indeed the central, the innermost doctrine of Christian freedom, marred indeed for us by the expressions of divine wrath and legal satisfaction which are used to convey the doctrine of redemption, but not marred by the conception of irresistible predestination into which his sense of the majesty and holiness of God and the worthlessness of man betrayed the extreme Calvinist. Moreover this passion for freedom directed Milton in more secular affairs. It inspired in the *Areopagitica* some of the noblest words ever written on the freedom of opinion, and, at the crisis of the Puritan revolution it made him turn to Cromwell against the Presbyterians in parliament to bid him—

> Help us to save free conscience from the paw
> Of hireling wolves.[2]

And when all was over, when Oliver was dead and the king restored, he wrote the last great tragedy, *Samson Agonistes*, which is the tragedy not only of greatness wantonly thrown away, but also of freedom negligently lost.

> But what more oft, in nations grown corrupt,
> And by their vices brought to servitude,
> Then to love Bondage more then Liberty,
> Bondage with ease then strenuous Liberty.[3]

By the side of Milton must stand Oliver himself. Oliver Cromwell is not an easy man to assess or to epitomize. He was the creature of a revolution, drawn from his natural orbit by a series of events that revealed in him a genius that might otherwise have fusted in him unused; by that genius he was carried to circumstances and urgent responsibilities for which neither preconceived principle, nor any ordinary experience could have prepared him. Therefore it is not to be expected that any simple

---

[1] Book III, l. 294.   [2] *Sonnet to Cromwell.*
[3] *Samson Agonistes*, l. 268. On Milton and liberty see F. E. Hutchinson, *Milton and the English Mind* (Teach Yourself History Series).

formula could cover his actions. Moreover, his is a great mind clouded by shadows, often guided rather by intuition than by reason and unconscious of its own subtleties, and often inarticulate, his utterances varying from the simple vivid strength of his most telling phrases to the strange rambling confusion of some of his more difficult speeches. It is a mind liable on occasion to be distorted by emotion which reduced him to tears or betrayed him into moments of black rage, and a mind sometimes tragically narrowed and shuttered by the circumstances of his age and time, as the crime of Drogheda shows. And all the while his eyes are always striving to see, beyond the drama being enacted in England, the realities of a larger more important drama, the drama of his salvation and that of other men, which was being worked out in a spiritual world which transcended but included the material, in which sphere it manifested its existence by signs and providences and mercies. Oliver is not an easy man to judge, yet if his career be fairly considered must it not be conceded that he was all the way through profoundly if at times obscurely concerned for the freedom of Englishmen, as he understood it and as circumstances seemed to permit? This is surely evident in his early struggles for parliament, in his wrestlings to win a satisfactory settlement from a complacently oligarchical parliament and an evasive king, and, when that was all over, in the constant attempts he made to provide his dictatorial rule with a parliamentary constitution. It is also shown in the very real religious toleration he allowed, again when circumstances permitted, toleration beyond the use of his time, even to the practice of creeds he could not understand like Anglicanism or Roman Catholicism.[1] Respect for freedom appears in his language throughout, and, despite the roughness of his actions or even the apparent craftiness, on occasion, of his policy, his life does not really belie him.[2]

Behind Cromwell were Cromwell's comrades in arms, organized in one of the most remarkable military bodies in the history of this or any other country. There is no space here to describe the extraordinary ferment that took place in that army when the issue with parliament was being discussed in 1647–49.

[1] W. K. Jordan, *The Development of Religious Toleration in England 1640–1660*, London 1938, pp. 144–253.

[2] Perhaps the best portrait of Cromwell is in John Buchan's *Oliver Cromwell*, 1934.

Nor is there need, for it has often been most ably analysed by historians, while in their pamphlets and manifestos and in the reports of their debates the actors themselves left most revealing records behind them.[1] But the record is remarkable. These men drew up the first scheme for the effective reform of parliament, they demanded religious toleration, while in the advanced political thought of their left wing they showed a concern for the rights of 'the poorest he that is in England' which is two centuries before its time. In all this the emphasis was on the freedom of the individual, and if the result was the imposition on the country, by force, of a rule which a large majority of the country hated and repudiated, that was more truly one of the usual ironies of history than the result of hypocrisy or the greed of power.

Now this concern for freedom was, in part, inherited by these men, almost unconsciously, as part of their secular legacy as Englishmen. Though they dissolved parliament by the sword they believed in some sort of parliamentary rule; though many of them particularly disliked lawyers and the law they were apt to believe in a fundamental law that should guarantee the rights of every man. It was also, in part, the direct result of the war, the feeling natural to every army that a man who has fought, be he private soldier or officer, has a right to enjoy that which he has won by his perils and much suffering, a feeling which this army was able to express with unusual effectiveness, because it was unusually articulate and had unusual opportunities of self-expression, and was unusually moved thereto by the action of its masters. It was also, in part, occasioned by the fact that in the army certain classes were well represented: small freehold farmers, tradesmen, weavers and the like, all of whom had grievances at the way society was conducted and were able to urge them in these very unusual circumstances in a way that was impossible for them at most periods of English history before the nineteenth century.

But behind all these factors was another which had helped to give the inarticulate tongues and minds of their own, had helped the army to discipline and success and united both private soldier and officer in one common bond. The most active among these men were Puritans, or at least spoke the language of Puritanism,

[1] See Sir Charles Firth, *Cromwell's Army*, ed. 1902; and *Puritanism and Liberty; being the Army debates, 1647-9, from the Clarke MSS., with supplementary documents*, selected and edited with an introduction by A. S. P. Woodhouse, London 1938.

and the fact makes it necessary to look more closely at that word
'Puritan'.

Though Puritanism plays a very important part in the development of the English heritage it is extremely difficult to give a
precise meaning to the word itself. It probably starts as a nick-
name or term of abuse,[1] it ends certainly as a piece of historical
jargon. It is applied to a very large number of different people,
and it is difficult to find a common denominator. In one of the
most careful discussions of the subject it is suggested that 'Puritanism means a determined and varied effort to erect the Holy
Community'.[2] Be that as it may one common denominator is
certainly a hunger and thirst after righteousness and the quest
for salvation. But it is that quest pursued under certain special
conditions and with certain particular presuppositions, with the
presuppositions in fact, revealing or limiting, which were natural
to the men of the Reformation.

The Reformation was, in one aspect, a revolt against existing
religious authority and existing religious practices, and the
Puritan tended to believe that the Christian Church after the first
few centuries had divagated into hopeless superstition and
idolatry and had become subdued by the corruptions of an
eminently unconverted world. Therefore he was inclined to
repudiate, more or less ruthlessly, what came to him with the
authority of any age after that fall had taken place. In the place
of traditional authorities he was apt to look to three things for
direction, to the Bible, possibly as interpreted by appropriate
divines, to the experience of the human soul saved by the blood
of Christ, and to the signs and testimonies by which God mani-
fests His will in history. But in all things that will must be
sovereign, and the zeal for purity which the Puritan's name
suggests had therefore best be thought not as a particularly queasy
attitude on matters which might have some relation to sex, but
rather as a general passion to purify all life and all religion of all
that was incompatible with the will of the Almighty, revealed
in the ways that he believed it to be revealed.

Even to epitomize so far is to over-simplify, and thereafter the
roads go far apart. For instance the Presbyterian found in the
Bible a scheme for Church government which was reflected in
the Presbyterian Church, but the Independent or the Baptist did

[1] See Richard Baxter, *Reliquiae Baxterianae*, ed. 1696, p. 32.
[2] Woodhouse, *op. cit.*, p. 37.

not believe that any such organization was part of the divine plan, and repudiated it vigorously as coming between man and his God. Or on another point, to the high Calvinist the work of salvation was for God alone, He alone could save, and therefore God in His inscrutable wisdom chose whom He would save, and damned whom He would damn; but there were many who could not accept this conclusion, and there were endless varieties of doctrine on the part man's free-will could play in his own salvation. Or again there was the controversy, which absorbed many minds in the seventeenth century as indeed afterwards, whether the baptism of infants was compatible with the facts of the New Testament or with Christian experience, or whether baptism should only be administered to adults who had received knowledge of the saving grace of God.

But in all this the emphasis was inclined to be on the individual. The scripture is to be interpreted by the individual, even it can only rightly be interpreted in a certain way; the experience of the saved individual soul was infinitely precious and revealing; the individual was the hero, or villain, of the drama of salvation, and a man who had passed, as very many Puritans had passed, through the agony of conviction of sin and the joy of conversion, knew that he had something which separated him personally from the rest of the world, which the world had not given him and which the world could not take away. That did not, of course, mean that the world would cease to meddle with the Puritan, or the Puritan cease to meddle with the world. The path of the pilgrim still lay unavoidably through Vanity Fair where he might with good reason expect ill usage, particularly since it might be his duty to testify against what he saw there, and fight against it if he could, even if the unconverted might in the hardness of their hearts have considered some of the things he condemned to be innocent or even laudable. But though he was in the world he was not of the world, and the claims of what only belonged to this world, the claims of kings, princes, parliament, carnal learning or ancient ecclesiastical authority could be lightly set aside by the man or woman who pursued or possessed the one thing needful.

Now it may be objected that though these things may provide a firm basis for freedom for the Puritan, they do not assure at all certainly freedom for anyone else. There is much in that objection, particularly since the spirit of the Puritan creed was, as has been said, not contemplative but active, inspired with a zeal for reform. This had its excellent side, particularly perhaps in the desire for social justice which it sometimes developed.[1] But it developed the fault of trying to impose by force a moral discipline which could only be of value if it were voluntarily accepted, the kind of activity which has at times made the English Sunday a day of rest and spiritual refreshment to those who could use it properly, but of gloom and desperation only to be mitigated by alcohol for those who could not. Moreover, the Puritans suffered from a sin which easily besets intensely religious people. Having found salvation by one road they could not believe that anyone was sincerely seeking it by any other, and they developed a lamentable tendency habitually to impute low and contemptible motives to their opponents, a habit of which their descendants in the nineteenth century, as well as others at that time in other religious parties, were not entirely guiltless. It is not a habit which encourages justice to those whose opinions you cannot share. Nor for that matter did meditation on the fiercer parts of the Old Testament, nor the sick apocalyptic dreams of ignorant fanatics breed at all naturally a spirit of mercy towards those who could be conceived to be idolators or opponents of the rule of the saints.

But in considering these matters it is important not to include all Puritans in the same facile condemnation. For instance it is not true to say, as is sometimes said, that the Puritans concentrated all their reading and meditation on the Old Testament. They did read the New Testament as well, indeed as was natural they were drawn to St. Paul to whose experience and doctrine they owed very much, and the message of St. Paul is pre-eminently one of liberty, liberty from the law, liberty from the flesh for those who being dead with Christ are risen with Him. Nor obviously did they neglect to read the Gospels. It is true, as is also true of other dead Christians, that some of the lessons which they thought that they had derived from that source may seem to us a little odd, but it is clear that there were those among them who did learn the lesson of mercy and charity as well. In fact, as ever, the Bible proved a starting point from which men could journey in many different directions.

But, as well as this, on certain theoretical issues which were critical in the history of freedom, the Puritan bodies diverged very

[1] See W. Schenk, *The Concern for Social Justice in the Puritan Revolution*, London 1948.

widely indeed. The Presbyterian Church was one that claimed to control the whole country, and though it restricted salvation to the elect it applied discipline to all. This meant that Presbyterians made no breach in the old tradition of one Church for the whole country working in close alliance with the state, from which the individual diverged at his peril. But the sectaries who made the most vocal part of Cromwell's army were apt to deny the authority of any larger unit than the separate congregation, Baptist or Independent or what you will, in which the elect were gathered. Into such a congregation they were unlikely to accept the unconverted and so far from wishing to use the power of the state to compel men to come in, they were apt to deny its right to interfere in any way with religion.

This indeed was a very important development, on which the later Noncomformist position was largely founded, and which, as will be seen, has its relevance to the problem of the undenominational state. But its importance in the seventeenth century was that it led the sects to the doctrine of religious toleration. Probably the first body in England to teach that doctrine were the 'General' Baptists.[1] The Congregationalists followed suit and so in due course did Cromwell's army. There was perhaps a certain tendency to restrict toleration to other varieties of Puritanism and to deny it to prelacy and popery, that is, the religions of the majority of their fellow countrymen. But in the circumstances it was natural that men should have their limitations; and as has been said Cromwell's own standard in the matter was a very high one. There is some evidence that not all of his followers reached it. What Puritan rule would have been without him we shall never know, for it did not long survive his burial in Westminster Abbey. Nevertheless it was after it had failed, and because it had failed, that the Puritan Revolution performed its greatest services for freedom. Puritan rule provided the nation with a straitjacket the nation did not want, Puritan 'Dissent' or 'Nonconformity' did something much more valuable.

After 1660 the defeated and oppressed cavaliers regained power and started to persecute the sectaries and the Presbyterians, because they were afraid of them. But though after the restoration the Dissenters were chastened, they were not destroyed. They remained faithful to their beliefs, and in due course the com-

[1] T. Lyon, *The Theory of Religious Liberty in England, 1603-39*, Cambridge 1937, pp. 109 *ff.*

munity had to come to terms with them; while the sufferings and courage of the Quakers in particular helped to make all religious persecution odious. Other currents both in secular society, and in the Church of England itself were flowing towards the same end, but it was the perseverance of the Dissenters after 1660 that more than anything else secured that after 1688 a modified toleration became part of the law of the land and of the English tradition.[1]

But a mere rehearsal of the course of history will not fully reveal the significance of Puritanism in the English heritage. What is of permanent living importance is not what it did, but what it was. What it did is finished, and, as with all things in history, must in the view of men seem partly accidental. What it was was something which had an important part to play after the seventeenth century, possibly has yet an important part to play; for it relates to the permanent problem of the position of man in the universe.

In the Puritan scheme of things man simply as man was in a position of supreme importance; and by that word man was meant not a composite abstraction but every man, woman, and child. It might be that the destiny of human beings was decided for them by the inscrutable will of an omnipotent Creator, or it might be that they were involved in a cosmic drama in which they were free even to disobey, but the grand issue was the same. It was individual salvation that mattered, not the future of the race, the greatness of the nation or the creation of some earthly Utopia for the conquest of which certain existing individuals might reasonably be considered to be pawns. It was an issue to be worked out in the separate person of every child of God, and by every child of God. Before that issue the convenience of states, the customs of society and the awfulness of earthly power shrank into insignificance.

Of course that view is, or should be, common to all Christians, and that is why both Reformation and Counter-reformation were able to challenge the growing power of the state in the sixteenth and seventeenth centuries. But the Puritan to a peculiar extent had to work out his destiny alone. He had the Bible and the Cross as his guide, but he normally lacked the help of a traditional

[1] For religious toleration in general see T. Lyon, *op. cit.*, and W. K. Jordan, *Development of Religious Toleration in England*, Vol. I, to 1603 (1932), Vol. II, 1603-40 (1936), Vol. III, 1640-60 (1938 and 1940).

creed or the consolations of a trusted Church or the encourage-
ments of a sympathetic society to take some of the burden off his
shoulders. He had left those things behind in his pilgrimage. It
was not like a man going his way with the genial sunlight of a
summer's day revealing a familiar and friendly landscape, but
like a man travelling in a strange country and on a dark day, lit
by one fierce ray of the sun breaking through the clouds, a ray
which singled him out and left inky shadows all round. There is
much to be said against that view of man's destiny, against the
losses it may cause, or the arrogance it may engender, but it has
its advantages; and of Puritanism in general one thing at least
must be said. It gave strength, it enhanced personality. In that
dark country and in that bright light a man must stand up to his
full stature, even if he also knows that without that light he
himself would be in utter darkness.

Perhaps that enhancement of the human personality was most
important and significant when that ray struck down through the
crust of society and illuminated relatively unlettered men and
men in humble station. Bunyan's *Grace Abounding* is one of the
most interesting documents of the seventeenth century; interesting because of the long, heart-rending struggle through which
Bunyan passed, with on the whole only the Bible as guide, before
he found peace, but it is interesting also because it is the record
of a way in which an uneducated working tinker developed until
he was capable of being the author of *The Pilgrim's Progress*; and
beside that story one must place the story of George Fox, the
son of a Leicestershire weaver, who became the founder of the
Society of Friends. It is indeed very well worthy of thought to
consider how little society gave to these men and how great is
their stature in English history; but it is also important to turn
from the men of exceptional genius to the rank and file, to
the soldiers of Cromwell's army, to the yeomen, craftsmen,
husbandmen and shopkeepers who are to be found in the lists of
the first Quakers,[1] and to consider what the Puritan Revolution
made of them. If part of the realization of freedom is, as it is, the
liberation of human beings from the natural effects of restricted
circumstances, limited education or lack of economic privilege
and the like, then surely that is precisely what the Puritans did for
these people; and it is difficult to conceive any other agency that
would at that period have done the same. So far from religion

[1] E.g. see Ernest E. Taylor, *The Valiant Sixty*, 1947, p. 42.

being the opiate for the people, it awakened them, and made men.

There is in the *Reliquiae* of Richard Baxter, one of the great Puritan divines, a passage which gives an interesting picture of some of the classes to whom the new message came in the seventeenth century. He is speaking of the reasons for his success in the town of Kidderminster. 'And it was', says he, 'a great advantage to me that my neighbours were of such a trade as allowed them time enough to read or talk of holy things. For the Town liveth by the weaving of Kidderminster stuffs; and as they stand in their loom they can set a book before them, or edifie one another; whereas Plowmen, and many others, are so wearied and continually employed, either in the labours or in the cares of their callings that it is a great impediment to their Salvation; Freeholders and Tradesmen are the strength of Religion and Civility in the Land; and Gentlemen and Beggars, and Servile Tenants are the strength of iniquity (Though among these sorts are some also that are good and just as among the other are many bad).'[1] The picture is of a message which came home to the self-respecting working men and working masters,[2] but which did not so often appeal to the gentry who had competing traditions or to the more self-confident 'rich' who, so Baxter said, would 'not endure the due conduct of the ministry'; and also not to the 'beggars', the people who were not so steady and not so industrious, or of course to the 'drunkards', or to the 'rabble' of whom Baxter elsewhere has cause to complain.

But if the humble and meek are exalted, they may not remain meek. In this feeling about beggars there is moral danger. It was a very natural feeling. The steady hard-working man does not find it easy to endure the toss pot and the idler, nor the serious man those who make a mock of his endeavours. Nor was it easy to be indifferent to the scoffers for there were obviously many people in the towns and villages of the seventeenth century who objected for very human reasons to the airs which the Puritans gave themselves, and showed their objections in concrete form when they had an opportunity. But though these feelings are natural they are dangerous; steadiness, sobriety and hard work are apt to breed wealth; drinking and idleness and throwing stones and dirt at the neighbours on the whole do not, and in a world divided as sharply as was that of the Puritan into the godly and

[1] Baxter, *Reliquiae Baxterianae*, ed. 1696, p. 89.
[2] Baxter, *op. cit.*, p. 94.

H

ungodly there was an undoubted temptation to note with complacency that the godly were apt to prosper and that the ungodly often did not. It was a danger that probably increased as the first fervour of Puritanism wore off and the descendants of the Puritans settled down to the sober business of making their living in trade or industry, a business at which perhaps they were sometimes a thought too successful.

To this tendency to canonize industry and even perhaps wealth, which was the obvious reward of industry and sobriety, must be added something else. The development of Puritanism coincided at least in time with the partial breakdown of some of the ideas and authorities which had in the past given some order and restraint to economic forces. The stringency of the condemnations of usury was abandoned and the naked power of money increased, while such control of the economic sphere as had been exercised either by ecclesiastical authority or royal prerogative broke down. Now the Puritans became prominent in the business world, indeed many were so from the start, and they certainly were prominent in the revolt against Church and king. It has therefore been laid to their charge that they played a part, a major part, in the production of a world in which there was little to discipline the ruthless forces of capital and commerce in the name of morality and humanity, and in which business success was counted as virtue, and poverty as vice.

As is well known this problem of the relationship of Puritanism, and for that matter Protestantism as well, to contemporary economic and social developments has received the careful attention of many scholars.[1] It ought to be said that it is a very difficult problem. It is difficult partly because it is intrinsically difficult in such matters to be clear what is cause and what is effect, and to decide whether the development of a particular set of religious beliefs facilitated certain contemporary developments, or whether any religious beliefs at a certain period would have been in part affected in the same way by the economic forces which were developing in that particular society. It must be remembered that there were Roman Catholic capitalists in the sixteenth century and high capitalism in certain countries long before the Reformation. It is also difficult to sum up, fairly, the

[1] See R. H. Tawney, *Religion and the Rise of Capitalism*, London 1926; M. Weber, *The Protestant Ethic and the Spirit of Capitalism*, transl. by T. Parsons, London 1930.

economic and social morality of any period, and to compare it, fairly, with the economic and social morality of another. Moreover, if such comparison is made with the object of testing the value and effectiveness of Christian ethics under different systems and at different times, it should perhaps always be made over the whole field, and consideration given to the relation of the Christian Church to such things as the inequalities and brutalities of feudalism, or the demands of absolute monarchy, or the moral failures of a landed gentry, since the most important question at any given moment would seem to be the extent to which religion accommodated itself to what was dominant and conventionally accepted rather than its capacity to condemn what may have been weaker and, for the time being, more exceptional. It may also be suggested that the economic morality which was taught, say, in the eighteenth century has not yet been satisfactorily fully examined and summarized; certainly the condemnation of usury was not entirely dropped, you can find it for instance in a sermon preached by a famous nonconformist divine in the middle of the eighteenth century, though it might be said that his definition of usury was not sufficiently stringent.[1] Moreover the difficulty is increased by the fact that the word 'capitalism', which is often used in this connexion, is not a word which is always defined accurately; nor is it always clear at what point that word sums up satisfactorily what is most important in the prevailing economic relationships between man and man.

The subject is a difficult one, too difficult to be discussed here; but unfortunately it has obscured in many people's minds the true value of Puritanism in the national tradition. However, it has done this not only because of its intrinsic difficulty, but also largely because the conclusions of the scholars who have written on the subject have been taken over and caricatured by enthusiastic religious and political propagandists, who have seen in the matter no difficulties at all. Worse than that, they have been apparently simplified for the purpose of teaching in the schools, so that those whose lot it has been of late years to examine schoolboys have sometimes received from the babes and sucklings a very dreadful picture of Protestantism or Puritanism as being wholly motivated by a desire to keep the loot of the monasteries, to charge 20 per cent. on usurious loans and to ensure the triumph of 'capitalism', with the companion definition that 'capitalism'

[1] James Foster, D.D., *Sermons*, London 1744, Vol. III, p. 313.

was something very wicked invented by Puritans or Protestants. It is difficult to believe that a boy or girl who has been suffered to believe such rubbish can think justly about something which has been important in the past, and may be important hereafter.

For the moral of the early political history of Puritanism and Protestantism is surely this: whatever their defects, whatever their relation to the forces of commerce, or capitalism, or what you will, Puritans and Protestants helped to secure the freedom of mankind. They did this in part because they formed part of the great religious revival, which taught men, through both Reformation and Counter-reformation, to resist the powers of the secular state in the name of something more important. But Puritanism has also this particular importance in English history. It produced human beings who were capable of working out their own freedom, however meagre the inheritance with which society had endowed them. Whatever its limitations it made men, and I will try to show that the same beliefs, the same traditions, could repeat the process among the proletariat in the conditions produced by nineteenth-century industrialism. In addition to this, Puritanism also produced a tradition which denied the right of the state to interfere with matters connected with religion. But to the history of that, also, I must turn in the next chapter.

Here, however, one generalization may be hazarded. Does not this history perhaps suggest that secure freedom, or even to use a dangerously obscure phrase 'true' freedom, is not something which can be conferred by law, or by tradition or by birthright or even perhaps by the social service state, but must be something whose sanctions are outside the reach of society, however benevolent society may be? It may even be suggested that the power to obtain it must come from within a man, or perhaps from above. But if those last words are true it cannot consist in doing just what one likes, even if what one likes is not peculiarly inconvenient to one's neighbours.

VIII

RELIGION AND LIBERTY—THE DISSENTERS IN THE EIGHTEENTH AND NINETEENTH CENTURIES

'The great God who gave us all reason and conscience never appointed the conscience, nor the reason, nor the will of one man absolutely to appoint the religious duties of another.' Isaac Watts, A New Essay on Civil Power.

THE early eighteenth century was not on the whole a happy time for Protestant Dissenters. They were tolerated but no more, indeed until the famous case of Allan Evans, not completed till 1767, it was not clear that Nonconformity had so much legal warranty as to enable a man to plead it as a defence in the Courts.[1] Their remoteness from fashionable society, their exclusion from many of the prizes of life were enough to incline the cold-hearted among them, were they wealthy or ambitious, to drop off.[2] Moreover it was a time when many hearts were growing cold. The flames that had burnt so fiercely in the seventeenth century flickered down and sank. Religion grew too often safe and tame, to be valued primarily for its exposition of morality. Too often it stiffened into a rather lifeless orthodoxy, or was translated into a rational creed, which was tempted to reject the old view of the divinity of Christ. This movement towards Unitarianism, or what was loosely called Socinianism, affected both Church and Dissent, particularly in what had been the leading Dissenting body, the Presbyterians; and, in the period immediately before the French Revolution, the two leading Dissenting Ministers, Drs. Richard Price and Joseph Priestley, were both Unitarians. Small wonder that there was a tendency among eighteenth-century Dissenters to inquire into the reasons for the 'decay' or the 'low state' of the 'Dissenting interest'.

[1] Anthony Lincoln, *Some Political and Social Ideas of English Dissent, 1763–1800*, Cambridge 1938, pp. 45–6.

[2] Priestley, *Works*, Ed. Cit., Vol. XXII, p. 289. An Address to Protestant Dissenters (Chapter 'On the Low State of the Dissenting Interest').

Actually if they could have known it the future was to be much more prosperous. England was on the eve of great developments in her economic structure. Commercial wealth and industrial wealth, which was often in the hands of Dissenters, was to increase greatly, progressively reducing the preponderance of the landed interest which was normally closely allied to the Church of England. Many of the leaders thrown up by what is called the industrial revolution were Dissenters, so that in the nineteenth century Dissent was going to be able to claim a very much larger share of those who were powerful and wealthy in the land.

Nor was, in the long run, the course of politics to be unfavourable, with one very serious setback. The death of Anne meant the end of the Tory attempt to go back on the toleration achieved at the Revolution, and the Dissenters hailed George I and George II as deliverers, and till the death of George II were ostentatiously loyal to the Court. With the accession of George III and with the developments that took place in English politics between 1760 and 1770 there came a change. The movements which in the end were to open the gates to the great Whig Reform Bill of 1732 and the progress of the nineteenth century were beginning, and many Dissenters were drawn into them. According to Priestley there were many Dissenters who supported George III until the government interfered with the elections of John Wilkes in 1769 but then went into opposition, though not, he says, influenced in this by opinions peculiar to Dissenters.[1] Certainly the war with the American Colonies caused many Dissenters, several of whom had fairly close connexions with the Colonists, bitterly to oppose the king and support the Americans; while the movement for parliamentary reform which also started in the '70s gained strong Dissenting support. Indeed the period between 1770 and 1790 was a time of rather sanguine hope. The times were stirring, to many Dissenters, and not only to Dissenters, it seemed as if it was high time to awake out of sleep, for at least the earthly regeneration of mankind was at hand.

In fact it was a prologue to the nineteenth century, and even so it was disappointing. The corrupt electorate was not reformed, even though William Pitt himself as Prime Minister proposed a Bill for that purpose. The Dissenters made strenuous efforts to get their worst disabilities removed, but they failed to convince parliament; and then the curtain was rung down abruptly by the

[1] Priestley, *op. cit.*, Vol. XXII, p. 355.

French Revolution. When the Revolution started it seemed, rather naturally, to many Dissenters that here was the true dawn of all that they had desired for mankind, and they welcomed it with enthusiasm. But the Revolution pursued its course into tumult, bloodshed and war, the reaction in England was violent, and the Dissenters were trapped. Dr. Price's famous sermon triumphing over the early stages of the Revolution was the subject of Burke's bitter wrath in his much more famous *Reflections*. Priestley's house and laboratory in Birmingham were burnt by a Church and King mob, and he ended as an exile in America. Reform was at a stay, and what had happened confirmed for many the old thesis of the fundamental disloyalty of the Dissenters, and the subversive nature of their principles. As a result the bitterness between Church and Dissent was intensified, parliament built churches to counteract Dissenting influence, and further restrictive legislation was threatened against them, though happily not passed.

It was a miserable reverse, but it was after all only a temporary one. The work of reform in England was delayed but not stopped by the French Revolution. In the new century it went forward with increasing impetus as soon as the Napoleonic Wars and their immediate aftermath were over. In 1828 came the long desired repeal of the Test and Corporation Acts, in 1832 came the first Reform Bill which gave Dissent increased political strength. One by one the special disabilities were destroyed, the difficulties about the marriage and burial of the Dissenters, the bar to the universities, the bitterly felt grievance of church rates all in due course disappeared. The work was unconscionably slow, it went on into the second half of the nineteenth century, for the Church's privileges, even when they were valueless, were stubbornly defended, which was indeed natural since what was being attempted was in fact a fundamental change in the structure of the state. Nor was this change ever successfully completed. Many Dissenters earnestly desired and ardently worked for the disestablishment and disendowment of the Church of England, indeed there were many Dissenters who felt that that was one of the most important issues in nineteenth-century politics, but they were never successful. But even if you take full account of all these delays and disappointments, the transformation of the Dissenters from the despised and restricted Dissenting interest of the eighteenth century to their nineteenth-century condition was amazing, amazing not only in what was done, but in the increase of power it symbolized.

The Dissenters had not only vastly increased in wealth, they had also vastly increased in numbers. The figures of the various religious bodies at different times are the subject of controversy, but it seems to be probable that in the second half of the nineteenth century Dissenters of all kinds almost equalled the numbers of the Church of England.[1] They were strong in the great new cities, and they were stronger than is usually believed in the countryside, and with their numbers, and with the political development of the country and the extension of the franchise, their political power increased. It is true that they never completely controlled the Liberal party, indeed in the '70s they became grievously disappointed with that party because of Forster's Education Act, and partly because of Mr. Gladstone's opposition to their motions for disestablishment. But they seem to have been swept back into the ranks of the Liberals by Gladstone's crusade against atrocities in the Turkish Empire, most, not all, of them were in favour of Home Rule, and after the great Liberal triumph of 1906 there were more Dissenters in the House of Commons than ever before. But by then the position was undermined.

Now it should be realized that the importance of the part played by Dissent in these political developments was not only the result of their numbers, but also of their principles. What may be called 'liberal principles' were in some sort the logical development of Dissenting principles, and were widely propagated by Dissenting teachers. In the eighteenth century possibly the best systematic political education that was given in the country was given in the great Dissenting Academies of which mention has been made. In moments of temper and of crisis these remarkable places were naturally accused of being nests of rebellion and hives of sedition, which they were not; but they helped to teach principles in politics, the importance of liberty, the right of the people to enforce a change in the system of government where that was necessary, the desirability of a more accurate system of representation, which made men ready to take their part in the general movement for reform. Of course these principles were not peculiar to Dissenters. They could be

[1] W. G. Addison, *Religious Equality in Modern England, 1714-1914*, London 1944, pp. 99-103.

derived and were derived by others from the same traditions and literature as those from which the Dissenters themselves derived them. Many people who were not Dissenters had in their libraries the writings of such old republicans as Algernon Sidney and Milton, almost every educated man read John Locke, and very many people followed the development of thought on the Continent. But there was one principle of particular importance to the theme of this book which the Dissenters had made peculiarly their own.

Since the beginning of the eighteenth century the Dissenters had had to justify their separation from the Established Church of the country, and this they did in a variety of ways. The day of wrath in Dissenting history was St. Bartholomew's Day in 1662, when the ministers who had held livings in English parishes during the Commonwealth were extruded if they were not prepared to accept certain conditions.[1] Naturally the Dissenters denied the propriety of those conditions, particularly that of episcopal ordination, learned arguments against which can be found in the first part of a book which many Dissenters considered to be the best statement of their position, Edmund Calamy's *Defence of Moderate Non-Conformity*. But they also grounded their case on general principles. They denied in the name of the freedom of the Christian conscience the right of authority to enforce any 'impositions' on the conduct of worship, and attacked as impositions on the individual conscience the use of a fixed liturgy, the requirement that communicants should kneel, the use of the cross in baptism and such like.[2] And they went further. To support that plea they denied the right of the state to enforce anything at all on Christians which was not necessary for the proper performance of that duty which they held to be the sole object of the state's existence, the duty of maintaining an orderly secular community. These arguments can be found in the Introduction to the second part of Calamy's *Defence* published in 1704. There, dealing with the well-worn scriptural admonition that we must obey the higher powers for conscience sake, he says, 'But still if the Prince and the Bishop, the Parliament and the convocation join together to require what

---

[1] For a discussion of problems relating to this ejection see C. E. Whiting, *Studies in English Puritanism from the Restoration to the Revolution, 1660–1688*, London 1931, Chapter I.

[2] Calamy, *Defence*, Part II, ed. 1704, p. 20.

God hath neither subjected to the former nor submitted to the rule of the latter an obligation to Obedience is wanting.'[1] This denial of all but a limited authority to the state could be made to include most of the things to which Dissenters objected, to the use of public money to support the teachers of any particular form of religion, or to the imposition of civil incapacities on those who dissented from that form, as can be found in an *Essay on Civil Power in Things Sacred* written by another eminent Dissenter, Isaac Watts, the writer of hymns.[2]

Obviously the force of this argument came from the conception that the powers of the state could not rightfully extend beyond what was necessary to secure the objects for which it was founded, and that these objects were in general only what might be called police objects, the maintenance of order, the protection of property, the organization of prosperity and the resistance of foreign foes. With other matters, either because they were matters of indifference, or because they were matters of conscience, the state ought not to meddle.[3] This view was not peculiar to Dissenters. In theory a very constricted conception of the objects of the state was common in the eighteenth century, and in fact the English state was hardly trying to do more than the Dissenters prescribed, and failing to do as much. Indered here was a danger that those who pleaded for an established Church and were anxious to enlist Christianity in the service of the state too often degraded religion also into being merely an agent for police purposes, something designed to keep unruly people in order. Nor did the Dissenters find it easy to leave wholly behind the old idea that some sort of moral agreement on the essentials of religion was necessary for social order, and they were inclined to boggle at the admission of atheists, or even Roman Catholics, to complete political equality, while Watts provides in his *New Essay* a rather peculiar and perfectly unworkable scheme for the public provision of teaching about legal and moral duties.

But their agreement with other contemporaries, or the limitation or variety of their views should not disguise the fact that the Dissenters' very existence, and the grounds of their protest, constitutes a profoundly important revolution in the whole conception of the nature of the state and the nature of its powers.

---

[1] Calamy, *op. cit.*, p. 72.   [2] Watts, *Works*, ed. 1753, Vol. VI, p. 135.
[3] Calamy, *op. cit.*, 2nd Part, pp. 24 *ff*.

In the old view, which might with some exaggeration be said to have prevailed since the conversion of Constantine, the state had so to speak an official knowledge of what was supposed to be true and an official duty to support it. This the Dissenters effectively denied, and in their eyes the establishment of, at least, religious truth must be left to the conscience of individuals. Priestley sums up their position by saying: 'We think it best that there be no uniformity in matters of religion except a *perfect freedom of enquiry.*'[1] It follows therefore that in matters relating to religion (and who shall say what matters concerning truth or belief do not relate to religion?) it is better that the state should be, as far as is compatible with the needs of order, neutral, an umpire to hold the ring in which all men, unfettered and unfavoured alike, will work out their differences by discussion. It was an idea that had been approached by certain seventeenth-century Puritans, but the facts of the eighteenth-century state with its highly privileged Established Church did not correspond with it, nor perhaps do the facts of the twentieth-century state, for Priestley also says: 'that Education is a branch of civil liberty which ought by no means to be surrendered into the hands of the magistrate: and that the best interests of society require that the right of conducting it should be inviolably preserved to individuals'.[2]

However, any dilemma which that sentiment might in time present to Nonconformists was remote by nearly a hundred years. In the late eighteenth century Dissenting thought was peculiarly well suited to a generation whose idealists were more intent on liberating man from the corrupt institutions which had enslaved man rather than on devising institutions that should actively improve him. Indeed in the spirit of optimism and assurance which then prevailed it could be generalized into a doctrine with no sectarian theological preoccupations. To quote Priestley again: 'But whatever the views of Dissenters originally, though they were extremely narrow and confined at first they have so long been the weaker party, and consequently in an interest opposite to the views of tyranny and arbitrary power; that at length, they have begun to understand their situation, and have found the true and just principles on which the cause of *universal-liberty* may be best supported.'[3]

[1] Priestley, *op. cit.*, Vol. XXII, p. 37.   [2] *Ibid.*, p. 54.
[3] *Ibid.*, p. 263.

He was thinking in this passage of the intolerance of the old Puritans, but his mind went further than theirs in other directions, for one of the liberties which Priestley claimed for himself and for others was liberation from formularies imposing the doctrine of the Trinity, and though it is true that much of his work pre-supposed the existence of God, and he himself obviously made much use of the Bible, no theological assumptions at all would seem to be necessary to enable a man to accept that view, which he deemed to be his great discovery, that the object of the state is to secure the 'happiness' of the individuals composing it, an idea from which Jeremy Bentham is said to have drawn inspiration.[1]

In fact these 'true and just principles of *universal-liberty*' were able to coalesce with other strands of eighteenth-century thought that had little or no relation to orthodox Christianity. From that body of thought have developed certain ideas which do not appear to need, in fact can be opposed to, the Christian hypo-thesis. They are roughly these. Man's rights and liberties can safely be grounded not upon any eternal law, or the decree of any divine legislator, but upon the tendencies and potentialities of his own nature. Give those free play, prevent them from being thwarted by exterior circumstances, and he will find his way to the happiness which is the natural object of his existence. A system of government which really represents the wishes of the people will not produce wars, an economic system in which men really understand the identity of their interests will need no exterior control. The conception of freedom has broadened down from a rejection of the authority of the state in certain particulars to a practical disbelief in the necessity even of divine authority in anything at all.

Sometimes this line of thought has appeared in the full blown, fully realized, doctrine of the perfectibility of man, more often perhaps it has hovered undefined at the back of men's minds and inspired hopes, sometimes very noble hopes, from the eighteenth century to the present day. It has inspired many Christians some-times to their best efforts, but at its most sanguine it is a little difficult to combine with the ancient Christian doctrine of original sin. For one of the marks of this line of thought has often been great self-confidence, a self-confidence which often descends

[1] For a short account of Priestley's views, see Lincoln, *op. cit.*, Ch. V, pp. 151 *ff.*

bravely from the general to the particular. Men have felt that if you could only remove this or that particular obstruction to the development of man, this corrupt form of government, that oppressive economic system, then man will assuredly settle peaceably in the promised land, the machinery of coercion will no longer be needed, the state will wither away. Yet, alas, the history of all that self-confidence has been full of disappointments. The corrupt unrepresentative governments of the eighteenth century were cleared away, and yet there were wars; the restrictions on the free play of man's economic interests were removed, and yet there was oppression; while the systems that have replaced free capitalism have so far been notable rather for the strictness of their control than the generosity of their liberty. And the obvious answer to each disappointment has been to create machinery to control more narrowly the presumed cause of it, till men march towards the promised land in huge highly disciplined battalions. In fact in some cases so iron is the discipline that it rests very largely with the conscience of the commander whether they continue to march in the direction in which they set out.

Nor has that self-confidence seemed to satisfy the most intimate needs of large sections of mankind. It is a notable fact that whether or no Priestley represented tendencies in political thought that were to brood over the nineteenth century, his own theology, which had appeared to be in the obvious line of progress, was not to predominate in it. The Unitarians were to be important in the nineteenth century, in some ways they were to form an intellectual aristocracy in the ranks of Liberalism and Dissent, while the Unitarian tradition of enlightened social service as it appears say in Birmingham or Leeds is one of those facts whose great importance historians have yet to realize. But other bodies among the Dissenters also produced important intellectual leaders, and it would seem to have been other bodies which developed the great numbers and had the greatest popular appeal.

For another tradition also emerged in great strength from the eighteenth century. If one looks back on the whole immense and varied achievement of English eighteenth-century literature one can, I think, say with some confidence that three relatively short pieces of verse have meant more to more people than anything else, and they are not to be found in *Lyrical Ballads* and Gray's *Elegy* is not one of them. They are three hymns, 'Rock of Ages', by a Calvinistic clergyman of the Church of England named Toplady, 'Jesu, Lover of my Soul', by Charles Wesley, and 'When I survey the wondrous Cross', by Isaac Watts, an orthodox and towards the end of his day rather old-fashioned Dissenter. To them should probably be added a fourth hymn, 'Our God, our help in ages past', also by Watts; but it would be hard to find anything else which could compete. They have been familiar to many people who have never heard of Priestley's name and were innocent of any knowledge of Jeremy Bentham. They have been sung repeatedly in every kind of place of worship from Westminster Abbey to the most desolate little Bethel in the most distressing industrial slum. They have been sung at disasters in mines, on the battlefield and on the decks of sinking ships, for they have often been of use to men and women faced with probable or certain death, as well as to others in less critical circumstances.

They do not breathe a spirit of self-confidence or, to any remarkable extent, of optimism. Take for instance the third verse of 'Rock of Ages':

> *Nothing in my hand I bring,*
> *Simply to Thy Cross I cling;*
> *Naked, come to thee for dress;*
> *Helpless, look to thee for grace;*
> *Foul, I to the Fountain fly;*

Or the second verse of Wesley's hymn:

> *Other refuge have I none;*
> *Hangs my helpless soul on thee;*
> *Leave, ah! leave me not alone.*

Or the last lines of the first verse of Watts:

> *My richest gain I count but loss,*
> *And pour contempt on all my pride.*

Yet it seems to be probable that it was these thoughts that captured the minds of far more men and women at least in the eighteenth and nineteenth centuries than the important doctrine of the perfectibility of man.

Of course that can be explained. Men and women with small cultural resources and faced with cruel external conditions have a morbid need to appeal for personal support from something, or more probably someone, outside themselves. Viewed fairly, it may not seem that that explanation adequately covers all the facts, neither the large variety of the persons who felt this need, many of whom had reasonable culture and adequate reasons for self-confidence, nor the effect on the lives and conduct of many of those who made this appeal, nor the general belief that from somewhere or from someone there was often a response. But without venturing on these difficult psychological and philosophical problems, it can at least be asserted as a historical fact that one of the most important and influential events in English eighteenth-century history was the great Evangelical Revival which taught not the value of the capacities of man but their inadequacy, the doctrine not of progress but of the Cross.

The most important agents of that movement were of course John and Charles Wesley and their friends, and George Whitefield, but they found already in existence both in the Established Church and in the Dissenting bodies many of the theological ideas that they used, and the revival had its important results both in the Church and in the older Dissenting bodies as well as among the people called Methodists. Indeed it is convenient to consider the revival as dividing into three main streams.

First of all, in the Established Church there was the Evangelical movement which managed to accommodate itself to the organization of the English Church and did very much indeed to renew its life. It left some very deep marks on the English character for it gave force and direction and leadership to some of the most important movements of practical reform that there have been. Through Wilberforce and the Clapham Group it gave force to the anti-slavery crusade, which was indeed of world-wide importance, through Lord Shaftesbury and others to the movement for factory reform and other social reform at home.

Secondly there was the middle stream, the 'Wesleyan' body proper, a new body in English life of great importance, which contained many people whom no religious body had affected before. They were lost to the Church, but retained a far more friendly attitude towards it than was derived from the old Dissenting tradition. Moreover Wesley left them a political tradition, which was either non-party or Tory, to which they were held in the first half of the nineteenth century by their great 'Pope', Jabez Bunting, with much controversy and some difficulty because the undertow towards Liberal politics was great.

Partly as a result of these difficulties and partly for other reasons other Methodist bodies developed on their flank, such as the Primitive Methodists, who are all worthy of study.

The third stream flowed in great volume into the old Dissenting communions themselves. It is true that at first many of the older Dissenters shrank from the Methodists, they did not like their ways and, with some reason, distrusted the emotionalism and the hysteria which were the froth of the movement. But they could not avoid catching fire, and it is probably as a result of this more than anything else that they were able to play the part they did in the nineteenth century. The incidence of the increase in their numbers is significant. There were three great Dissenting bodies in the eighteenth century: the Presbyterians, the Independents or Congregationalists, and the Baptists. In 1772 there were probably about 380 Independent congregations, fifty years later there were 799; and in 1772 there were about 390 Baptist congregations, fifty years later there were 532.[1] Moreover there is evidence that the individual congregations were larger, while these figures only represent a stage in a movement which had not yet reached its climax. Only the Presbyterians did not increase in numbers, which is significant, for the Presbyterians were the communion which above all others had been penetrated by those intellectual and philosophical currents of which Priestley may stand as the symbol. In fact it would seem that the new dispensation could only assist those who had retained the old theology and not tried to explain it away in the spirit of humanism.[2]

Now all this is probably of profound significance for the light it throws on the needs of the spirit of man, particularly on the needs which men felt most strongly at that moment in history, the time of the great romantic revolt against the rationalism of the eighteenth century. It certainly had very profound effects on the atmosphere of the England of the nineteenth century, and through that probably on the England we know. But it is well not to exaggerate its effects, at least on politics.

The Evangelical revival was not going to cancel men's belief in earthly progress, practical reform and democracy; in many cases it was rather going to coalesce with these hopes. It is true that what seemed to be definitely atheistical and godless in the

[1] R. W. Dale, *History of English Congregationalism*, 1907, p. 580.
[2] Bernard Lord Manning, *Essays in Orthodox Dissent*, London 1939, pp. 171 *ff.*, 'Congregationalism in the Eighteenth Century'.

French Revolution repelled men under the influence of the Evangelical revival, and that the loyalty of the Wesleyans during the crisis of the Revolution was probably an important factor in securing the stability and security of the country. But the fact that the old Dissenting bodies had been reinvigorated by the Evangelical revival did not make them change sides. The fact that a man has confessed himself to be a sinner and has learnt that he must look to the Cross for his salvation by no means carries with it the consequence that he must tolerate unjust and inequitable political treatment from the hands of other sinners. Even if he believes that the final destiny of man is to be settled elsewhere, that is no reason why he should not hope that things would be much better in terrestrial matters under a more representative government, or with a freer economic system, particularly if he is a successful manufacturer. It is true that their history for a considerable period inhibited the Wesleyans from joining the Liberal political movement, but the cases of such men as Alexander Kilham and Joseph Rayner Stephens showed the difficulties of holding that position.[1] Even if there had been no secular hopes and grievances to draw such men as the Dissenters were into politics, the privileges and position of the Established Church made it unavoidable that they should enter that field.

Indeed, in the second quarter of the nineteenth century a blast of hatred against the Church of England blows across English politics like a blast of hot scalding steam when the cock of a boiler is opened. In 1834 Stephens, one of the Wesleyan dissentients, prophesied that: 'Ere long the very existence of the Established Church would be like a tale that was told and remembered only for the moral evils which it had brought upon the Country.'[2] In 1841 Edward Miall, the Congregationalist, writing of the Church said: 'the whole thing is a stupendous money scheme carried on under false pretences; a bundle of vested rights stamped for the greater security with the sacred name of Christianity'.[3] Or in another passage he made the case that the State Church was the nurse and patroness of war. 'Trace', said he, 'the history of this or any other state Church, and almost every

---

[1] E. R. Taylor, *Methodism and Politics, 1791–1851*, Cambridge 1935, pp. 72–5, 149.

[2] George Smith, *History of Wesleyan Methodism*, London 1864, Vol. III, p. 203.

[3] Arthur Miall, *Life of Edward Miall*, 1884, p. 62.

I

footstep plashes in the blood of man.'[1] Of course it is necessary to remember that this was an excitable emotional period in English history and one moreover when many people from ministers of religion and members of parliament down to humbler people like Mrs. Wilfer enjoyed the use of a richly histrionic style. But there was real bitter smouldering emotion behind these phrases. It was the evident danger to the Church which that hatred threatened that launched the Oxford Movement. However, that movement with its suggestion of priestly power and the smell of Rome that hung about it, only added to the heat. It is true that in the later nineteenth century, when the lines of English society were blurred and the old grievances reduced, tempers were more genial, but you can feel to the end the old tension in the words of Dr. John Clifford, the great Baptist leader. In fact, wherever the guilt may lie, and the Established Church must take its full share, hatred was part of the legacy that Christianity bequeathed to England.

That hatred was further inflamed by the very fact that many of the leaders of Dissent and very many of their followers were deeply and continually involved in secular politics. Certainly if they are true to their mission the leaders of Christian Churches must intervene in politics, but they always do so at their peril. The most spiritually minded man in secular politics must have adversaries and he must have allies and he must have a policy. It is difficult for him not to put forward his policy as the undoubted will of God, even though it be partly founded on disputable secular calculations. It is difficult for him not to canonize his friends and even their secular interests.

He may be too convenient to his friends. Since the time of Balaam practical politicians have realized how useful can be the services of a minister of a religion who can be persuaded to pronounce upon their adversaries. It was not forgotten in the nineteenth century. For instance in 1838 Cobden who, with Bright, was one of the most effective of the leaders in the agitation against the laws which imposed a duty upon imported corn, noted that an agitation against those laws would have most success if 'a moral and even a religious spirit' were 'infused in that topic'.[2] The matter was attended to. The services of a man called George Thompson who might be described as a specialist in

---

[1] Miall, *op. cit.*, p. 66.   [2] Morley, *Life of Cobden*, Popular Edition, p. 126.

moral agitations were obtained, and in 1841 a meeting of about seven hundred Dissenting ministers of religion was assembled at Manchester who were asked by Cobden to declare that the Corn Law was 'Opposed to the law of God, was Anti-scriptural, and anti-Christian'.[1]

Now everyone concerned in this matter was probably completely sincere. They all believed, probably wrongly, that the Corn Laws were responsible for the sufferings of the people in the hungry forties, and, probably rightly, that they were supported by the selfishness of the landowners, who had also persuaded themselves that their interests corresponded with those of the country. But it was possible for conscientious people to differ on the practical effects of the Corn Laws. It was not clear to everyone what effect their repeal would have upon wages, while many firmly if erroneously believed that their repeal would devastate the country districts. Without condemning any of the participants it might perhaps have been better if such heavy spiritual artillery had not been brought to settle these issues, and if it had not been originally directed by manufacturers whose first grievance against the Corn Laws was that they restricted their chance of trade.

Nor is it easy for the most spiritually minded man in politics to be just to his opponents. One of the springs of action in politics is organized enmity, and as a result politics is apt to hold up to the eye of the beholder a distorting mirror in which it is difficult to discern the motives of the images which pass for men on its surface. Or rather it is too easy, your friends are good, while the motives of your opponents are highly questionable. To take another example. Shaftesbury looking back on his struggle to reduce the hours of labour in factories noted that the Quaker John Bright, a man who dealt much in spiritual issues, 'was ever my most malignant opponent',[2] and anyone who takes the trouble to read Bright's speech on March 15th, 1844, will understand what that adjective means.[3] Now it was possible at that moment for a conscientious Christian to oppose legislation

[1] I have learnt the remarkable history of Cobden's relations with George Thompson from an unpublished thesis by R. English, Scholar of Trinity College, Cambridge. For the conference, see Prentice, *History of the Anti-Corn Law League*, London 1853, Vol. I, pp. 235 *ff*.

[2] Hodder, *Life of Shaftesbury*, 1886, Vol. II, p. 210.

[3] *Hansard Parliamentary Debates*, Third Series, Vol. LXXIII, 1,132.

which aimed at the reduction of the hours of the factory labour of children to ten, it is difficult for us to believe that but it was so. Moreover, Bright thought that Shaftesbury was probably using his cause to delay the repeal of the Corn Laws, which he believed was the measure which would most help the factory workers. But none of this really condones in the circumstances the tone of moral superiority and the insinuations Bright used against Shaftesbury, whose motives were really about as pure as a politician's could be. To explain that and to be just to Bright, it must be remembered that Bright saw not the real Shaftesbury and the real problem but Shaftesbury's image and that of the whole question in the distorting mirror of acute party divisions.

Indeed it may be claimed that the nineteenth-century Dissenters saw too much in a mirror that distorted the features of their fellow countrymen. The distortion came not only from party politics, but from real grievances reasonably resented, from anger at social privilege and the insolence of class, and from the old Puritan vice of imputing base motives to the other side and dividing the world sharply and inaccurately into the godly and ungodly, a habit which even at this day has descended on several who would not recognize its ancestry and have abandoned the creed which originated it. The results were unfortunate. This intimate mixture of English politics and English religious divisions probably made both more bitter than they need have been. It also probably helped to introduce into English politics that tone of satisfied self-righteousness and of facile condemnation, that tendency to moral hyperbole, of which Balfour complained in his famous, and most brilliant, open letter about Dr. Clifford.[1] But these tones and tendencies have been by no means confined to the Dissenters, indeed they have gone to make up that famous English hypocrisy of which Continental writers complain. But it is not hypocrisy in any simple sense. In Dissenters, and in other Englishmen, it has been rather caused by an intense desire to make moral judgements on practical affairs without realizing to the full how difficult moral judgements in practical affairs really are, and the profound examination of his own motives to which a man must subject himself before he makes them.

For behind all this there was in truth an intense passion for national righteousness. The descendants of the Puritans still truly

[1] Arthur James Balfour, *Essays and Addresses*, Edinburgh 1903, p. 415.

desired to erect the holy community. You can see this in the passion for temperance, in the fires kindled by Gladstone's campaigns against the Turks, in the anger which some Dissenters felt at the South African War, and even in the condemnation of Parnell's adultery. It is not necessary to believe that the Dissenters were right in the line they took on all these issues, but they were unquestionably sincere. It was indeed the same passion which made the English undertake the crusade against slavery, and the result of that crusade for the world demonstrates how inexpressibly valuable the desire to introduce moral judgements into practical politics may be. But it is morally at its finest when men realize how difficult it is to be practical and, the related problem, how very difficult it is to be just.

Therefore English politics had a considerable effect on the Dissenters, and the Dissenters a considerable effect on the English politics. How great an effect it is not possible to say, for no one can conceive English politics without them. Without them there would have been undoubtedly some movement to destroy the corrupt forms of government of the eighteenth century, it would probably have been in part Deist or atheist, the rift in the nation might have been deeper and more fundamental and the Christian religion more heavily compromised than it was as the defender of wealth and reactionary power. But all this is particularly empty speculation, unreal because so much of the English political tradition as we know it is the result of the history of Nonconformity and of Puritanism. The Liberal tradition owes much to the Dissenting tradition and looks back through nine-teenth-century democrats and economists to eighteenth- and even seventeenth-century Nonconformist sectaries and divines, while from the Puritans as also from the effects of the Evangelical revival in all denominations there probably springs that desire to conceive politics in terms of morality which has had both good and bad effects on the way the English look at things.

But it would be unfair to think of the Dissenters only in terms of politics, certainly only in terms of Liberal politics. Many Dissenters were not primarily concerned with political questions. Much of their most important work was non-political. Their work for foreign missions was all important, particularly that of the Baptists who were most courageous pioneers, and so was their work in the evangelizing of England. In the eyes of many men Spurgeon, the great preacher, was a more important man than most members of parliament, and in the eye of eternity many humbler pastors probably more important than Spurgeon. As with the Church so with Dissent the most important work was done in regions where we cannot follow it, not in liberalizing politics but in the saving of souls, not at Westminster but in the hearts of men. It is not possible to calculate the results, but it is possible to see something very significant.

It is sometimes said that Dissent in nineteenth-century England was predominantly middle-class.[1] That may have been true of many religious bodies, or of congregations within those bodies, it was not true of all. For instance it was in all probability not true of many Baptist congregations, and it was not true of the Primitive Methodists of whom Hugh Bourne a carpenter and William Clowes a working potter were the originators. Certain sections of Nonconformity were not only active among the working classes, but they also gained much from working-class initiative and leadership. That was indeed their strength; the story of Dr. Clifford demonstrates how a man who started under the harsh conditions of a child labourer in a factory could rise through nonconformity to a position of great importance as a religious leader. The same spirit that had made men in the seventeenth century was reaching down into the ranks of the under-privileged in the nineteenth century and performing the same task.

As in the seventeenth century so in the nineteenth, that fermentation had its effects in other fields than the religious. George Loveless, the agricultural labourer who is one of the martyrs of the early Trade Union movement was a Methodist preacher, so was Joseph Arch the founder of the Agricultural Labourers' Union later in the century. The autobiography of Thomas Cooper gives a vivid description of how a Methodist preacher became a Chartist leader: indeed the whole question of the relation between Methodism and the advanced popular movements of the nineteenth century has furnished matter for interesting study.[2] As interesting would be the problem, which still awaits research, of the relationship between Nonconformity and the later Trade Union and working class movements, which could for example be studied in the career of Mr. Arthur Henderson who

[1] See Miall, *op. cit.*, p. 151.
[2] See R. F. Wearmouth, *Methodism and the Working-class Movements of England, 1800–1850*, Epworth Press, 1937.

rose to a high position in the Labour movement and the state. There was, of course, another working class tradition, the tradition of Tom Paine, of Holyoake, of the audiences who listened to Mrs. Besant in her earlier phase or to that courageous man, Charles Bradlaugh, a tradition which was apt to see in Christianity an enemy to the emancipation of man. But there can be no doubt that the debt of both the Trade Union movement and of the Labour Party to popular Christianity is both broad and deep. The management of the affairs of the Chapel gave to many men their first most valuable experience in the practical conduct of democratic organization, but the Chapel gave much more than that. It gave self-respect and a belief in a meaning in the universe in conditions where both were very hard to maintain. To quote Mr. Jack Lawson, speaking of his own experiences and the life of his fellow miners: 'The Chapel gave them their first music, their first literature and philosophy to meet the harsh life and cruel impact of the crude materialistic age. Here men first found the language and art to express their antagonism to grim conditions and injustice.'[1]

As with Cromwell's troopers so with nineteenth-century miners: religion taught the inarticulate to speak their grievance. Of course it may be said that it was the grievance that mattered, and that matters to us, and that the religion is of secondary importance; that it was natural that men should speak in the vernacular of their times, in the seventeenth century in the language of Puritanism and in the nineteenth century of pietism, but these facts are historical curiosities and of no contemporary significance. Yet if they are only historical curiosities they are at least curious. But are they only historical curiosities? It is possible to be too cavalier in one's treatment of what men apparently believe their own motives to be, for it is a standing temptation to start historical analysis from the hypothesis that people do not really mean what they say. Very many of these people thought that they believed that the most important problem was the problem of salvation, their own and other people's. Of course there were hypocrites among them, men like Mr. Stiggins and Mr. Chadband, for the language of piety was easy to copy, and there were comfortable parlours into which it could win an entry, and much pineapple gin, or its teetotal equivalent in good food, which it could earn. But it is not to be

[1] J. J. Lawson, *A Man's Life*, 1944, p. 69.

suggested that these worthies were concealed social revolution-
aries biding their time. More to the point perhaps is the case of
Victor Grayson, for a brief period in the twentieth century one
of the greatest Labour orators, who managed to use the Dissenting
facilities for relatively advanced education, though his interests
seem to have been entirely political. Still as far as one can judge
the matter there seems to be in fact little doubt that to very many
people in harsh conditions religious issues were profoundly real
and absorbing, and indeed were the most important issues in life.
The fact is worthy of some consideration.

Of course that does not mean that they were not interested in
social and political problems as well. There is nothing particularly
spiritual in assenting to what you consider to be economic
injustice, and at least a case for believing that it is your duty as a
Christian to do your best to remove it. Religion in England had
always had a tendency to be practical. The Puritans were practical,
the Society of Friends has always been very practical, so was and
is the Salvation Army. The Dissenters had always been interested
in practical social reform, for it must be remembered that the old
policy of *laissez-faire* economics and of freedom had commended
itself to many of them as a policy that would effect the most
important social reforms. That belief may have been mistaken but
it was none the less sincere, and not unreasonable; while there
were Dissenters who were active factory reformers in Shaftesbury's movement. Moreover, in the last half of the century many
Liberal Dissenters were turning to a more positive policy of
social reform. You can see that in the life of R. W. Dale of
Birmingham, in the activities of Hugh Price Hughes and in the
activities of the Liberal Government of 1906 of which that eminent
Dissenter Mr. Lloyd George was the driving force. It was just
as natural for practical Wesleyans to go into the work of Trade
Unions or of the Labour Party when that developed. It was a
natural and inevitable development from a spiritual point of
departure.

Nevertheless, for most practical Englishmen there is always
the danger of materialism. To believe in the very great importance of material things is not materialism, it is common sense;
materialism comes when you come to underrate the importance
of what is spiritual. The cause of this change of values may be
the fact that you have learnt to disbelieve in the existence of the
spiritual, but its more common cause is not so much a shift of

belief as a shift of interest. The practical business of the world takes up so much time, the problems presented by the good which might be procured or the evil which must be prevented become so absorbing that direct interest in what is spiritual begins to fade. In due course the importance of spiritual issues seems to be solely derived from their probable effect on the material world; people are to be virtuous that they may better serve the needs of your policy, not because virtue has any inherent value in itself. It is a process which is bound to lead to a general decadence of spiritual values, and leads also to a proportionately increasing belief in the absolute effectiveness of practical measures. In fact it also leads towards that secular belief in the perfectibility of man, which has beckoned to modern man ever since the eighteenth century. But the shift in interest can easily turn in time into a shift of belief. What you never think about comes by a natural process to seem to be less and less worthy of attention, its existence less probable, its propositions more contrary to that common sense which is too often the limited teaching of a man's own normal experience; so that when men do look up for a moment from their practical jobs, and their new amusements, they find that the old vision has fled, and they do not regret it.

Perhaps something of that sort happened in England. If one passes through the streets of many an industrial town one sees derelict chapels; they are turned into workshops, or garages, or offices, or warehouses, but it is easy to see what they were once, the centre of piety, the focus of what was most important in life, for some group of English people. In some cases no doubt the reason for their abandonment has been a movement of population, but in many cases it is the symptom of something more serious. In the late nineteenth century the increase in the members of the Dissenters began to slacken off and in the first decade of the twentieth century it turned into a decrease.[1] It was the mark of a change in the mind of the nation which affected both Church and Dissent. It was in part a change of belief with an intellectual explanation, but it was in large part caused by a change in habit, it was a change in the interests of people who did not even bother to change their beliefs.

Meanwhile men's secular hopes shone brighter than ever. There was so much to do, there was so much that could be done,

[1] E. Halévy, *A History of the English People*. Epilogue, Vol. II (English Translation, 1934), pp. 74–5.

much to be done by the Trade Unions coming into their own with much more powerful organizations than they had ever commanded; much to be done by the community, as was proved in the activities of the great Liberal Government which between 1906 and 1914 laid down the social policy which all twentieth-century governments were to follow; and much to be done by science which had enormously increased man's control over nature, if not over himself. Much could be done and much was done. You have only to look at the photographs of some of the old streets that still existed in 1900, or at the photographs of the children you would find in these streets, both at their clothes and at their faces, to realize how much has been accomplished, if the task is yet terribly incomplete. Small wonder that the old sanguine voices started to whisper more incessantly than ever. If only you can get rid of nationalism, if only you can get a real league of nations, if only you can get rid of capitalism, if only you can organize better education you can certainly find your way into the Utopia which lies just over the next ridge. And even if the way proves to be longer, more hazardous, more disastrous than those voices suggest, they express not ignoble hopes; and if they urge man towards a juster society, that direction is the right direction.

But as has already been suggested, there are various things to be considered as we follow in the armies of this secular crusade. There are the problems already discussed of the state whose law has become will, even if it is the will to social reform. Then there is the danger of those whose whole mind is set on improvements for the future and not at all on eternity. Eternity is now as much as it is fifty years hence, and its values are to be experienced and respected now. But the future is only the future and if it is the future which is primarily important, what may be valuable only at this moment in time may without compunction be sacrificed for what shall come hereafter; even if it is the lives of people who could only live in the present. Then if this Utopia is to be a place where the old dreadful dilemma between freedom and authority has disappeared, that might be because it is freedom which has disappeared, since men are not to be permitted to diverge from the convenient social pattern. For at the moment social betterment seems always to demand not less coercion but more, and the creation of even more complicated and more formidable secular organizations. After all the residuary legatee of all social enthusiasms has so far invariably been the secular state.

How impossible it is for men of goodwill to avoid that conclusion may be seen if we turn back to the history of the Dissenters, to the story of their policy in relation to public education, which seems to have produced a change in their theory of the state. It may be remembered that Priestley believed that education must never pass into the hand of the magistrate. Something like that position was maintained by Dissenters in the first half of the nineteenth century. It is true that they had special reasons for objecting to the system that prevailed. The system of grants made for the building of schools after 1833 so worked out that many more Church of England schools were assisted than non-denominational or Dissenting schools, because the Church was able to raise more money on its own behalf. The abortive educational proposals of 1843 seemed to put too much power of control into the hands of the Church and caused a very angry agitation. There was a standing and bitterly felt grievance that, in many districts, a Church of England school was the only one to which a little Dissenter could be sent, which was naturally a particularly sore point in a village where the school might be rather heavily overshadowed by squire and parson.

But for many Dissenters this was not a question of particulars, it was a question of principle. For instance in 1843 Edward Baines, a leading Congregationalist, declared: 'I am compelled to declare my opinion, that it is *not* the province of a government to educate the people; and that the admission of the principle that it *is* its province would lead to practical consequences fatal to civil and religious liberty.' He went on to argue his point and it is interesting to note that among his arguments was the old one of the restricted objects of the state: 'the proper province of government', said he, 'is to make and administer the laws, to protect person and property, and to conduct the external relations of a country; but that it is *not* its province to train the mind and morals of the people, any more than it is to supply them with food, or to govern their families'. Undoubtedly his opinion was sharpened by immediate controversy and informed by current conceptions in economics and politics, but it is remarkably like the views Calamy advanced in 1704.[1]

The principle was widely held, it finds its way as a minority opinion into the report on popular education that appeared in

[1] R. W. Dale, *op. cit.*, p. 659; cf. Calamy, *op. cit.*, Part II, p. 25.

1861.[1] It presented however this difficulty, it was completely impracticable. An attempt was made to develop schools without government support, but many Dissenters had from 1833 accepted grants for their schools, and had canvassed the proposal to provide secular instruction controlled by the ratepayers from local rates. In fact it became increasingly obvious that education for all could only be provided by public money. In 1867 even Edward Baines had to capitulate, and in 1869 a group which contained such eminent Dissenters as Joseph Chamberlain the Unitarian and R. W. Dale the Congregationalist founded the Educational League which demanded that the government should provide a system of education for the whole country which should be compulsory, unsectarian and free.[2]

Now there can be no doubt that the Educational League were right in pressing the need for education subsidized by the community, which should be both free and compulsory; and as little doubt that they were perfectly loyal to the nonconformist tradition as they saw it. The freedom of conscience was to be protected by democratic local control, and by the prohibition or segregation of sectarian or denominational teaching, which it was held should be done as far as possible out of ordinary school hours, in the home or in the church or chapel or Sunday school. Yet the fact that they were clear-headed, faithful and sincere only adds the significance to the fact that at least there appears to be here a profound revolution in the opinions of Nonconformists as to what activities might legitimately come within the province of the state.

In order to consider that matter it is fortunately not necessary to adventure among the thorns and brambles of the educational controversy. Among those thickets there were, and are, many very difficult particular problems, as for instance whether the undenominational teaching of Christianity is of any value, what should be the fate of denominational schools already in existence, what protection should be given to the conscience of the teacher

---

[1] 'The minority admit that the responsibilities and functions of government may be enlarged by special circumstances and in cases where political disasters have retarded the natural progress of society. But they hold that in a country situated politically and socially as England is, government has, ordinarily speaking, no educational duties, except towards those whom destitution, vagrancy or crime casts upon its hands.' 1861 Command Paper XXI, p. 298.

[2] R. W. Dale, *op. cit.*, pp. 669–73; F. Smith, *The Life and Work of Sir James Kay-Shuttleworth*, 1923, p. 159, note.

or what protection the children should have against that conscience, and what is the value or should be the limits of local democratic control. Over all those issues the religious wrangled interminably and very angrily, presenting a spectacle unedifying before God, and infinitely wearisome to men. But behind these particular issues there looms the great problem of the right of the state to control the minds of its citizens. It is not a problem that can be simply dismissed by the prohibition or segregation of denominational teaching in the schools provided by the community, for the teaching of science, the teaching of history, the teaching of literature can be made to bear on final issues almost as effectively as the teaching of the Church Catechism or the exposition of the Bible; indeed if the work is to be done properly it is probable that they ought to be made so to bear on them. Moreover it is likely that the matter is not less but more important now than it was at the end of the last century, when the instruction provided by the state was both meagre and elementary, and was more likely to be balanced by religious instruction in the chapel or the home. With each necessary step in educational advance the state takes greater and greater powers to mould the minds of the children, particularly of the children of the poor. Yet the central point of the old Dissenting position was the freedom of men's minds and consciences from state control; and who shall say with confidence that they were wrong?

There can be no going back to the old theory of the state, at least not to that held by the Dissenters. Nevertheless their history suggests something that may be needed to balance the new. For the history of religion in the sixteenth and seventeenth centuries suggests that no theory of the state nor practice on the part of the state can be fatal to liberty if men are seized of a freedom which the state can neither confer nor deny; and to such a freedom the histories alike of the Puritan revolution and of the Evangelical Revival point the way. Their roots were in the faith of the individual, their scene of action the experience of the individual, their sanction the responsibility of the individual. They were beyond the frontier of what can be controlled by kings and parliaments, yet what they did and felt profoundly affected the secular world, for round their history much of the history of English political freedom, and at least some of the history of English economic freedom, is ranged. Perhaps, indeed, that fact is significant. Perhaps it is safer in the end even for secular freedom to urge man to 'pour contempt on all his pride', and recognize some other sanction than his own urgent view of his own sovereign need.

But all this raises questions which cannot be considered apart from other factors in the English inheritance, and to understand them it is necessary to consider the fate of other constituents besides that of Dissent and how they also fared in the dissolving media of the nineteenth and twentieth centuries; and to those problems I turn.

IX

THE NINETEENTH AND TWENTIETH CENTURIES—THE FLUID SOCIETY

'For nowadays institutions are no longer habits as they once were, but ideas.' Frederick Temple, April 27th, 1848.

IT is still difficult to get the nineteenth century into historical focus. The scene is vaster, more detailed and less stable than ever before. Not only is England still part of Europe, which is still the most important vortex of life and conflict in the world, but she is now pre-eminently the busy crossroads of a world-wide trade and of a world-wide Empire. Even in England there are more people to be taken into account, there is more to be known about them, while the whole stream of life is more changeable and turbulent. Seldom have so many new forces been let loose on humanity in such a space of time. Indeed to try to summarize what is important in the nineteenth century is like trying to make a picture not of a stretch of a river, but of the whole Atlantic in storm, and trying to do so while still tossing on its waves. Of many of the forces liberated then we are still the playthings. Other centuries may be dead, but the nineteenth century is still alive. And no evidence for this is more eloquent than the fact that so many people are still in self-conscious affronted revolt against what they believe to have been the essentials of nineteenth-century civilization, particularly since the substance of the case for that revolt was formulated in the century itself, and many of the ordinary satiric points men use were concocted then.

Yet for all its revolutions the nineteenth century by no means cancelled all that had gone before. In fact, as a century it is remarkable for its survivals and revivals, and, rather markedly, for the survival and revival of Christianity. That, however, was not the only survival. In England the old constitution took a very long time to die, and the old social hierarchy never did die. It was in fairly vigorous health at the end of the century and is not dead yet, while what can be called the aristocratic principle, with all its advantages and disadvantages, received the reinforcement of a new and powerful supporting army.

The public schools as we know them were the invention of the nineteenth century. It is true that the history of many of them goes back beyond 1800, but fortunately the places we know bear little resemblance to what they were in the eighteenth century. Then they were certainly virile, very often much too virile, otherwise it is probable that eighteenth-century schools seldom had much to recommend them, except perhaps that they often succeeded by brutal methods in teaching some very unlikely boys no negligible command of Latin and Greek, thereby forming the basis of a common artistocratic culture such as we do not now possess. But Arnold and Thring and the other remarkable men who laboured in that field created something new. Their schools were more orderly and humane than the ordinary eighteenth-century school, they tried new methods and inculcated new ideals, and above all made possible a new aristocracy of the middle class. The very organized games they developed to take the place of the old country sports are a symbol of what they did, for the old aristocracy had very largely been an affair of country gentlemen living on paternal acres solaced by traditional amusements with their places in a traditional order headed by the landed aristocracy. Certainly it had always been possible for a man to buy a place in that society, which has constantly been refreshed by wealth acquired in commerce or industry, to the permanent disadvantage of those districts which may, after the industrial revolution at least, have been ruined to make the money. But to send a boy to a public school, and thereafter probably to Oxford or Cambridge, was easier, and cheaper. Once there he mixed with the sons of landowners, lawyers and clergymen and became without question a 'gentleman'; and if you study the social history of the middle and later nineteenth century you will find a good many manu-facturing and even Dissenting families which by this means were reconciled, or seduced, to the traditional social order of the country. Indeed it was probably this system more than anything else which helped to fuse together an upper class which was large enough and varied enough to stand the vicissitudes of the nine-teenth century.

In many ways this was unfortunate, particularly because the

basis of the public school system was not territorial. On the whole a boy went to the school which had a good reputation, or otherwise attracted his parents, and not if he could afford it to the school in the town of his birth or necessarily to a school in its neighbourhood. If he returned to work in his native place he was no longer quite a native of it, he spoke a different language from most of its inhabitants, had bonds of friendship which drew his mind away from its borders, and above all had not had with his fellow townsmen that close association in youth which is perhaps the closest neighbourly bond there is. Perhaps this helped to impede the development of that vigorous provincial life which England needed and still needs, and, worse than that, it helped to create a caste, to emphasize a horizontal social division, at a time of growing wealth and growing social tensions when a horizontal division was particularly dangerous.

Yet with all their disadvantages, their snobbery, the original narrowness of their curriculum, their harshness at times to exceptional boys, their exaltation of games, it would be absurd and mendacious to deny the public schools their virtues. The tiresome reiterations of portentous speech-day orators, and the sermons of exalted headmasters, about the tradition of service, the sense of responsibility, the code of honour must not disguise the fact that a readiness to accept the duties and the pains of responsibility was indeed very often taught; that there was a code of honour, if perhaps at the worst it sank down to the simple maxim that on no account must you give your friends away; and that there was even a tradition of service.

To all this England owes much. Of course much of what was best in the country not only never passed through the public schools, but would not have been so good if it had passed through them; and the public schools turned out much that was worthless with enhanced pretensions because it had their stamp. Yet there were many public school men who carried into life the standards and traditions which in part at least they had gained at school. The country has gained much from them in a good many different fields. The particular advantage of a middle class aristocracy is that it can be more pervasive than an aristocracy which is likely to be tied to one economic section of the community and to one set of functions. The public school boy was not so apt to be confined to the traditional aristocratic trades of war, government and the management of land, and in the work of government he

K

was willing to undertake relatively humble tasks. It is not for nothing that it was largely from the public schools, and from the reformed nineteenth-century universities which they fed, that a rather remarkably uncorruptible and devoted civil service was built up in the nineteenth century for Great Britain, for India and for the Colonies. Nor was this sense of active social duty restricted to those who were civil servants. In this matter perhaps their patron saint is Tom Hughes, the man who wrote *Tom Brown's School Days,* a typical and very attractive product of Rugby, one of the main authors of the whole public school legend, and at the same time one of the first Christian Socialists who spent much of his life in devoted service to the cause of co-operation. Following in his train is the devoted army of workers in school missions, organizers of boys' clubs, residents at university settlements, often less Radical and less coherent in their views than he was, but not entirely negligent of their duty to their fellows.

Of course there is another side to all this. There is a moral objection to all aristocracies. The greatest moral advantage of aristocracies is perhaps that they create a sense of personal obligation and responsibility which cannot be evaded or explained away or thrown on the community; the objection to all aristocracies is that, be they of birth, party membership, or education, they are all founded on inequality and normally present personal advantages which the unworthy are very ready to exploit. Moreover there is perhaps an objection to any system which relies as fully on the values of barbarism as did the public schools at their worst. But after all the public schools did not create the class system in England, nor yet the sharp divisions in wealth and opportunity among Englishmen; and as for barbarism, many men have made much worse use of the values and attractions of youthful barbarism than did even the silliest public schoolmaster whose mind hardly strayed from the football field or the cricket pitch. When the Devil makes up his accounts for the twentieth century, which it may be feared he will do with great self-satisfaction, he will be able to put the abuse of youth movements as a considerable item on the credit side, for one of his most successful ventures has been the exploitation of the generosity, the courage, the natural arrogance, the bodily prowess of young men and young women for evil ends by evil men. In fact such exploitation is easy, but the public schools never fell to the worst modern levels. Even the worst public schools were usually trying, often in a very muddled sort of way, not to organize barbarous evil but to turn barbarian virtues into Christian good.

For such moral strength as the public schools possessed, and it was at the best schools in the best periods a good deal, came to them very largely because those who made them and fostered them were Christians and very often Christian priests who regarded this work as their vocation. There has been much to be said with justice against public school religion. It has too often been deficient in intellectual quality, an appeal to loyalty and to sentiment instead of an appeal to mind, a reliance on the effects of an urgent appeal by the headmaster not to let the school down, followed by 'Lead Kindly Light' in the encircling gloom of the last Sunday of the Summer Term rather than on a satisfactory grounding in, say Bishop Butler's *Analogy*, before that moment arrived. It has also sometimes shown a strange tendency to get entangled with the values and disciplines of organized games, and it has sometimes been accused of not being Christianity at all, but Stoicism making use of Christian phraseology. Nevertheless, even Stoicism is not the most contemptible of all creeds, and it is none the worse for having a Christian top dressing: and after all much that has been said on this topic has been either ignorant or deliberately unfair. The public schools have often given men a personal creed that has been deep and lasting; and the work done by Christianity for English society through the public schools has been not the least valuable of its services to the English inheritance.

But the achievement of those schoolmasters was only a small section of the achievement of Christianity in the nineteenth century. It was indeed a most religious century. There was renewed life among the Nonconformists, there was renewed life in the Church of England. First of all the Evangelical revival and then the Oxford Movement helped the Church to awake from its eighteenth-century torpor. But historians have been prone to concentrate too much on those two movements. What is at least as important is the general improvement all round. From the time of Lord Liverpool onwards there seems to have been a better use of the Government's ecclesiastical patronage; the institution of the Ecclesiastical Commission started the work of internal reform that should have been started in 1529. Higher standards of professional conduct were developed among the clergy.

Among the laity there was probably a greater attention to religious duties, as is shown by the revival of family prayers. There was ceaseless activity in Church extension with the creation both of new parishes and new bishoprics so that a real attempt could be made to evangelize the whole country. In fact before the century ended the Church of England had changed beyond all recognition from the rigid humdrum Establishment of the eighteenth century; and this in itself was only a part of a larger whole. For there was the same vigour among the Dissenters; and the Roman Catholics, proscribed in the sixteenth and seventeenth centuries, sunken to a small remnant in the eighteenth century, now became, partly through conversions and partly through Irish immigration, an important part of the nation's life, producing at this time two of the greatest English Cardinals, Newman and Manning. Indeed even in the England of to-day you can see on every side signs of that great religious revival. You have only to look about you in the streets of most English towns and villages to be surprised at the number of churches and chapels built in the nineteenth century, as also, too often, to marvel at the badness of their flaccid Gothic, their brasswork, and their encaustic tiles and above all of their stained glass windows.

Now that bad taste may be significant. Of course its causes were complex, indeed to understand the whole question of that strange decay of taste one would have to look outside Britain and study the comparable art in Italy, in France and above all in Germany. But one of the causes of bad taste is mass production, and it is possible that nineteenth-century religion itself may have also suffered from mass production. The endless flaccid Gothic arches have their counterpart in endless flaccid nineteenth-century hymns. And then there are the popular religious pictures, particularly the pictures of angels in nightgowns, and the statuary in both Anglican and Roman Catholic churches, or to turn to another department there are the more melting examples of the religious and quasi-religious literature of the time.

Much of all this mass is only tasteless, facile and commonplace, but much is sentimental and some of it is very rich and lush indeed; and the impression it all gives is of something produced on a large scale for a very large public which has neither taste nor education to correct what it receives, nor always deep enough personal experience to give it the touch of reality. That is it is the product of mass production. Indeed one of the causes of sentimentalism is surely that it is mass produced sentiment, produced to extend the forms and pleasures of sentiment beyond the number of those who can be in the throes of any deep emotion. The matter is difficult because there were certain conditions in nineteenth-century literature and still more in nineteenth-century art which pandered to sentiment and bad taste whether they were mass produced or not. It can only be fairly judged when the popular religion of the nineteenth century has been carefully studied as it has not yet been studied. The appeal of its popular hymns should be analysed, as also the sermons of its most popular preachers and a study made of that popular religious Press which took such a delight in basting clergymen who showed any tendency to use vestments or not to believe in hell. When that has been done, a great deal that we now miss about the nine-teenth century will undoubtedly stand revealed.

But even without that research it would seem to be certain that nineteenth-century religion must have been affected as was everything else by the factor of numbers. It is probable that the population of Great Britain more than doubled its size between 1751 and 1831, and it is certain that it doubled again in the next sixty years. All the effects of this gigantic increase have yet to be fully assessed by historians, and its cultural effects were en-forced by another consideration. In the old world the culture and thought of the country were to some extent the privilege of the few. Now there were not only more people to make demands but many of them were more conscious of their needs and not a few were in a position to demand more. Swept away by the conditions of life from the custom and ritual supplied by the traditional life of the countryside for what these were worth, they needed a literature, an art and a philosophy which would suit them; and it is a tribute to the hold which Christianity had gained on the country, particularly since the Evangelical revival, that on the whole they still turned to the Christian religion, or at least to the forms, phrases and images of the Christian religion, to satisfy their need.

It was a gigantic and growing market and to meet it the nineteenth century applied its growing wealth, its great energy and its mechanical ingenuity. It produced the novelette, the cheap newspaper, and the oleograph. It produced the monster meeting, and the political agitation with a strong moral tang, and it produced Christian churches and chapels with ministers and

parsons to fill them by their hundreds. What it did not produce
in sufficient quantities was good formal education. There was a
surprisingly large amount of solid self-instruction, but it is quite
clear that that did not cover the whole ground, and what was
lacking, even for the middle classes let alone the working classes,
was good disciplined non-technical instruction. If we are to accept
the strictures of Matthew Arnold in that stringent book *Culture
and Anarchy*, it was very badly needed.

In these circumstances it may not be surprising that what was
produced was in some ways unsatisfactory, banal and uncritical,
at once very superficial and sublimely self-satisfied. But if this
is so, it may not so much prefer a criticism against the nineteenth
century in particular as draw attention to a serious problem of all
modern civilization. In the modern world the numbers to be
handled were probably far greater than ever existed in the world
before, and they had to be handled in a new way. In a stable hierarchical society what an ordinary man thinks about morals or about
the nature of the universe is supplied to him by either tradition or
authority. His mind and his actions are controlled by an ancient
creed which he does not question, which may also by its cycle of
rite, festival and public solemnity give meaning and even beauty
and gaiety to his life. In such a society independent thought may
be the function of a cultured and leisured class, whose leisure
supplies opportunity and whose background of taste and culture
supplies the critical power and historical perspective which is
probably necessary for such thought. Or independent thought
and popular guidance may be supplied by what Coleridge called
a 'national clerisy', a body like the clergy and the accepted learned
professions who can speak on matters of faith and morals after
both study and meditation, and will be attended to with respect
by those who well know that they have not had, and never can
have, the opportunity to dig for themselves in 'the mine of truth'.

But this situation is very naturally considered to be intolerable
by the modern man. Very naturally and properly he wishes to
decide things for himself, and he is told by flattering voices from
all sides that he is capable of doing so. Therefore he roughly
shakes aside the grip of tradition, and plunges into a swiftly
moving life in which the old cycle of rite and festival is difficult
and seems irrelevant. He rejects all authority that claims to do his
thinking for him; and in many ways he is right to do this, for free
thought is the mark of a free man, and the claim to intellectual

authority very often carries with it a claim to social privilege which is not conformable with a justly organized society. The problem, however, lies in the fact that the ordinary, or as he is now called, the 'common' man, may not realize how hard a task he has set himself, or how much he may lose or what dangers he may encounter if he does not perform it properly. And here the analogy of the Puritans, though they were rebels against the old hierarchy, may not be of much relevance. However poor and uneducated they were not normally examples of 'the common man'; they were exceptional men, the best of whom were acting under the impact of spiritual experience much more direct and immediate than is granted to most of us. Moreover, however much they were rebels they were expanding a traditional creed, which, to claim no more, contained within itself a wealth of past human thought and experience, of which they were heirs. But those to whom experience is denied and tradition is dead must gain what they need from education, and it is very import-ant to realize that the education which men need if they are really going to make the change from habit to thought, from authority to choice is not only very elaborate, but demands that the person to be educated should abstract from the urgent business of life more time and more effort than most people are prepared, or are possibly able, to give. Indeed it is one of the problems of democ-racy that it claims a freedom for the masses which can only be enjoyed after a preparation which cannot be mass produced.

But without that preparation and discipline a man may be rather apt to drift with the tide, to be at the mercy of impressions, of facts half remembered, of prejudices half-realized, of senti-mentalisms, of fashion, of clap-trap, of ill disciplined fears, of unreasoning dislike, of clichés, of all those things in fact which the modern science of propaganda exploits to the full. It may be difficult for such a man to forge for himself an adequate and secure system of principles to replace those which he has aban-doned, and therefore he may well be at the mercy of the appar-ently overwhelming importance of the needs of the moment, and of those who interpret those needs to him. In fact he may have ceased to obey the authority of the past and yet not have become free, ceased to be the heir of the ages and yet not the master of the future; and the sequel may be the triumph of forces as evil and as enslaving as those which took charge in Germany in 1933.

But if this is a serious modern problem it is likely that what

was unsatisfactory in nineteenth-century Christianity only represents what were the premonitory symptoms of it, for men can
be subjected to worse influences than the mass production of
what was at its lowest merely banal and complacent. In fact in
criticizing nineteenth-century religion there is some danger in
allowing aesthetic and literary taste, valuable as such standards
are, too great a part. Jejune phrases, mawkish hymns, grossly
sentimental pictures and what seems at first sight to be the most
miserable clap-trap may be the only way in which people in a
certain stage of culture can express sincere feelings of deep
religious content and ethical concepts which are acting as truly
valuable guides in life. It is necessary to study them with respect
to see what lies behind them, and in the nineteenth century it
would be probably unwise to trust that rather superior person
Matthew Arnold too closely as a guide to the nature of popular
nineteenth-century thought.

However, whether good or bad, much of that popular nineteenth-century religion was to wither away. As it was with the
Dissenters so it was with all. Fashion was to change, new amusements were to present themselves, and at the same time serious
intellectual opponents were to move into the attack and a time
was to come when it was to require hard thought and stubborn
faith to remain a Christian. Probably the change was in the long
run advantageous, certainly the test was severe. From a purely
intellectual point of view from about 1860 Christianity was
subject to criticism as searching as it has ever received, and where
it sprang from the claims of science it was criticism which the
conditions of life in the late nineteenth and twentieth centuries
brought home with force to a large number of people. Nor was
the defence of the theologians at the first onset particularly
impressive. The theologians were faced indeed with a task of
great difficulty, no less than a dangerous surgical operation.
Certain beliefs such as the literal historicity of the book of Genesis,
the old conception of what eternal punishment meant, had to be
excised; they were an encumbrance on the Christian religion but
they had for centuries been accepted as part of the Christian creed:
indeed to this day certain august authorities have not said frankly
or clearly what they think about them. Small wonder that many
either lost their faith or lost their confidence in it.

Yet all the time the business of life was urgent and the business
of thought remote and avoidable, and it may be questioned

whether the change was in every case one from blind faith to reasoned philosophy. Relatively few people have followed the controversy between religion and science along its subsequent course and considered the answers given by theologians after the confusion of the first onset. Relatively few have considered the criticisms by non-Christian philosophers of the assumptions of scientific materialism or naturalism, or the growing evidence for facts about the nature of human personality which appear to be inexplicable in the terms of that limited creed. Many did not even bother to renounce their nominal adherence to Christianity, they only abandoned the Christian view of the universe. In fact, in many cases the change was from one dogma to another dogma, if not more truly simply from prejudice to prejudice, with this difference, that the older dogma did present people with an orderly system of ethics and caused men and women to study one piece of great literature, the Bible; neither of which services has the newer dogma achieved. In fact the whole process as it affected a good many people may reflect little more than the flux and re-flux of fluid opinion, no longer directed by tradition, rightly liberated from authority and not yet controlled by disciplined thought.

However, whether the decay of nineteenth-century religion was advantageous or no, it still remains true that that religion had been a dynamic force in a changing world. No one could truthfully deny the depth and sincerity there had been in very much of the religion of the nineteenth century, nor the great strength and variety of the teachers it had produced, nor the importance of its practical achievements. Few centuries can have produced so many important and such different contributions to Christian doctrine, in few centuries can Christianity have had such important results for good on the practical conduct of secular affairs. The scene is world wide, it stretches over the continent of Europe, it stretches beyond. Indeed one of the greatest achievements is the success of the crusade against slavery, to which the English and the Scotch were in particular dedicated.[1] In 1807 they abolished their own slave trade, and in 1833 abolished slavery in the British Empire. They engaged their government in a difficult diplomatic campaign to outlaw the slave trade altogether. They placed expensive

[1] Sir Reginald Coupland, *The British Anti-Slavery Movement*, Home University Library (London 1933), and *Wilberforce* by the same author (London 1945).

squadrons of the British fleet on the west and east coasts of Africa
to catch the slavers on the high seas, and they turned inland into
the unknown fever protected heart of Africa to follow slavery
there, so that in the end the task was completed; and what was
completed was the abolition of an infamy, chattel slavery, which
had gone on since the beginning of history, and the ending, at
least in its worst form, of an age-old crime, the devastation of
Africa by Europe and Asia.

And then there were the missionaries, for this is the great age
of missionary expansion.[1] It has been customary to treat missionaries with contempt, or, if you were a historian, to neglect them
altogether: indeed scholars have pointed out that you get very
strange results if you try to find out about missionaries through
the index of such a work as the *Cambridge Modern History*.[2] Yet
both contempt and ignorance are obviously absurd. On the most
secular view this missionary expansion is an event of first importance in world history. With the trader and pioneer they penetrated everywhere, almost always at cross purposes with those
worthies. In England and Scotland they instructed a powerful
body of organized opinion which was apt to interfere violently
in public affairs in what it thought was the defence of primitive
races. Without doubt that opinion was often ill-instructed, self-
righteous, unjust and hysterical, and for all their devotion the
missionaries, with as little doubt, made mistakes. At first they could
not learn to understand or respect the traditional pattern of savage
life and probably put many thousands of men into trousers who
would have been much better without. Possibly, as often, they
removed the rude virtues of barbarism gaining only plausibility
in return. They very often quarrelled among themselves, and they
exported beyond Europe her ecclesiastical divisions, to be fought
even with the weapons of the flesh in some rather curious civil
wars in Uganda. Yet it is only fair to remember that their task
was very difficult, and that there is very much indeed to be put
on the credit side which is usually taken for granted and forgotten.
Indeed the whole question of the missionaries raises this important
problem.

In this century the rest of the world lay at the mercy of Europe.
Her arms were more powerful, her ships larger and swifter, her

---

[1] K. S. Latourette, *A History of the Expansion of Christianity*, Vols. IV, V, VI
(London 1941–3).

[2] Alan Richardson, *Christian Apologetics* (London 1947), p. 97, note 1.

commerce more highly developed than those of any other portion of the earth. That she would use this power to enrich the life of her own inhabitants was, and is still, historically inevitable and possibly historically desirable, but in what ways her power was likely to affect the lives and happiness of non-Europeans was, and is still, a question of the greatest importance, about which unfortunately many Englishmen have always refused to think without prejudice. In the last century European expansion was too often viewed with bland self-confidence and on occasion supported by an exuberant patriotism that could itself be the tool of some very ugly forces. Nowadays the pendulum has swung to the other end of its beat but not divagated into truth. The words which slip from the pen are 'exploitation' and 'imperialism'. Each word has at least two meanings and they are not normally used honestly. Exploitation can mean the development of a territory for the advantage of its primitive inhabitants and the world, or its enslavement simply for the purpose of gaining profit for certain Europeans. Imperialism can mean the extension of the rule of a foreign power over other men's territory simply to secure that enslavement, or it can mean, as it has often meant, its reluctant extension to prevent worse evils, among which exploitation in its worse sense by Europeans has ranked very high.

In fact the possibilities both for good and ill were great. European commerce could squeeze a territory dry and could do unmitigated evil, but it could also be the only way for a primitive people to escape from all obliterating poverty, and conditions which were no idyll of happy natural existence. It is not for nothing that both Fowell Buxton, the liberator of the slaves, and Livingstone himself saw in the extension of commerce and Christianity the best cure for slavery. The same contrast is true of imperialism. European rule when it was indolent, corrupt, tyrannical, or stupid could be simply an intolerable tyranny, but in many other cases it put an end to chronic oppression or periodical massacre picturesquely presided over by cruel superstition. There was both good and evil to be done, and no doubt both good and evil were done. Which has predominated is a subject worthy of objective study, but one must ask this question: given the lust, given the opportunities, given the arms what would have happened without Christianity, without indeed the organized exuberant Christianity of the nineteenth century? Of course, much of the good that European governments, particularly the British government, did was done not by the missionary but by the official applying decent standards of government and justice where they had not existed before, which in itself was in its way an extension of the Christian tradition. But in awakening the conscience of the country and in keeping it awake the various religious agitations at home, from the anti-slavery agitation on, were all important. And so were the missionaries who instructed those agitations at home and tried to serve in the field the interests of many who were certainly not strong enough or vocal enough to help themselves. In fact the real question is not what these people did wrong, but what would have happened if they had never existed.

But there is another case to be met. From the time that Wilberforce was attacked for caring about black but not white slaves, or Dickens reported Mr. Weller senior's unfortunate cynicism about the absolute value of exporting moral pocket handkerchiefs to young negroes, or Mrs. Jellyby's neglect of her children for the inhabitants of Borrioboola-Gha, the accusation has been made that all this seething hysterical interest in what was happening a long way off was a diversion, a hypocritical diversion, from duties nearer home. It may be that this criticism does touch on a quality in nineteenth-century Christianity which requires further study; certainly it was natural for men passionately interested in suffering at home to be angry with Christians whose eyes were on sufferings that were a long way off, and to feel not only that they were hypocrites, but that they ought to join in promoting those remedies which the complainants felt were the only cure for the evils of the time.

But though the feeling is natural it is not necessarily just. Suffering at home does not cancel the existence of suffering abroad, and it is morally dangerous to think it does. Nor were all the nineteenth-century Christians callous to what was happening at home; in fact it would be hard to point to any other factor which brought so many men and women to spend themselves in the service of the English poor. The Dissenting minister, the Evangelical lady, the slum parson, the soldier of the Salvation Army and the Roman Catholic priest and sister-of-mercy, were all drawn into a service that was a good deal more exacting than writing tracts on the evils of capitalism in the middle of the twentieth century. The service of some of these may not have been very intelligent, some of them may have been too much interested in individual conversions, or satisfied with the partial relief of individual cases, or their minds may at times have been darkened by the old belief that poverty was unavoidable and the order of society sacrosanct. But it is dangerous to judge other people's intentions by our sense of what is important, and it is simply not true to say that the minds of all nineteenth-century Christians were satisfied with pious palliatives. In fact several of them, because they were Christians, took part in what was the most important moral and intellectual revolution of the time.

The grand problem proposed to the nineteenth-century conscience was the problem of poverty. It was not new, but it was more obvious, more clamant, more urgent and more dangerous, and more nearly curable, than it had ever been before; but two conceptions prevented men from doing what they ought to have done and could have done to grapple with it. One was of course the ancient presumption that the distribution of men into different economic classes was inevitable if not providential; but the other thought was new and largely the result of the new science of economics. The laws of economic life were, it was held, now well known, and it was known that prices and wages and even living conditions were settled by the iron law of competition. For historic reasons the men of the early nineteenth century were in any case suspicious of government interference and apt to believe that all government expenditure was immoral, but it was now known, so they felt, that for governments to interfere with such things as wages, prices, and conditions of labour was like applying an ancient quack remedy to correct some well diagnosed bodily condition. It could not do good, and it might do terrible harm; for it was also known that there was an enormously increased population, a population whose increase according to Malthus always trod closely on the heels of supply. This was now supported by the titanic power of British industry. Allow that power to develop freely and the lot of Englishmen might continue to improve, hamper it and the result for many would be starvation.

What a humane responsible man should do when he is led by intellectually irrefutable arguments to morally intolerable conclusions is a problem on which professional moralists might further enlighten us, for a responsible man cannot evade the issue by saying that he will do good no matter what harm may ensue. Certainly the conclusions were morally intolerable. The harsh treatment of the unemployed, the aged, or the children, by the new Poor Law of 1834 was morally intolerable. The employment of children in factories for twelve, thirteen or even sixteen hours a day was morally intolerable. Yet so great was the authority of those arguments, supported as they were by some of the best minds of the day, that even a humane man like Sir Robert Peel, when Prime Minister, with the whole power of the state behind him, felt that he must resist his own party and limit what they wanted to do for the factory children. But of course not all men were humane, they never are, and selfishness, cruelty and greed were much encouraged by a law of nature which seemed to make it positively immoral to try to do good.

The position was morally dangerous, and it was socially dangerous; and in the 1840s the shadows were growing very long and very dark. Many of the working classes were bitterly discontented as was seen by the recurrent outbreaks of Chartism. Yet revolt was hopeless. The hopes of the Chartists were tragically absurd and their efforts futile. At that moment reform could only come from above, or it would come from nowhere; and for that to happen some men must be bold enough to challenge the teaching of the economists.

Fortunately for England that challenge was forthcoming. Already from very early in the century the sufferings of the children in some factories had been too much for some men to stomach and a series of, largely ineffective, laws had been passed to protect them; while many people were shocked at the methods of the new Poor Law when that appeared. No doubt many men were moved in these things by the dictates of simple humanity which it might be inaccurate to consider specifically Christian. But it is noticeable how many of the reformers in these matters appeal to Christian sanctions, and of how many it is true that the motive was directly derived in whole or in part from their religion. For instance, among the friends of the factory children this is probably true of Michael Sadler who was an important pioneer; it is probably true of Oastler, the factory king, it is true of Fielden, the Quaker, and it was pre-eminently true of Shaftesbury, whose primary inspiration was his Evangelical creed.

Particular reforms such as those for which Shaftesbury was responsible, and they were very many, were of course all important, but what was also wanted was a new theory both of economics and of the state, so that men might take a juster view not only of what the state might do, but also of what Christianity might tolerate. Such a theory was also forthcoming. In this matter the poet Southey was an important pioneer, and Shaftesbury learnt much from him. Southey's theory, and Shaftesbury's for that matter, was really an extension of the old conception of the order of society. Christian society had a paternal duty towards the poor which could not be evaded whatever the economists said. This was essentially a Tory conception, it is reflected in the generous romanticism of the Young England group in the '40s, as also in the pages of Disraeli's best novels, *Coningsby* and *Sybil*; and however useful it had a natural tendency to look backward to something which could probably never come again. More fundamental thinking was necessary to reach the conclusion that the task of Christianity was not to accept and spiritualize a traditional order of society but to transform it, not to make old conceptions of justice real, but new conceptions of justice possible.

Therefore probably the most important stage in the development of this matter was the appearance of another group of men in those tormented pregnant 1840s, the Christian Socialists.[1] Probably the most continuously important member of that group was a comparatively unknown man, J. M. Ludlow, but they were gathered round the theologian, F. D. Maurice, as their prophet, and perhaps their most influential orator was Charles Kingsley, the novelist, both of whom were in fact Church of England parsons. As a matter of fact their ideas gained another and even more powerful lay exponent later on, for from them, if also possibly from Carlyle, Ruskin drew the inspiration which led him to turn from the criticism of art to that of society and to write books which probably really did help to change the mind of the country.

The Christian Socialists attacked the iron law of competition as a lie, and strove to replace it with the principle of co-operation. To further this idea they spent much of their substance and time in promoting co-operative ventures, and did much to secure a change of the law, which enormously helped the development of co-operative societies. They got into touch with the Chartists, and worked in close association with the Trade Unions, and as well as all this founded and served the Working Men's College in London. Their practical experiments, except the Working

[1] See C. E. Raven, *Christian Socialism, 1848–54*, London 1920.

Men's College, on the whole failed, though it would seem that their contribution to the Co-operative Movement is greater than the Fabian historian, Sidney Webb, rather significantly, will allow. But even so none of their practical work, nor even their theoretical attack on the law of competition, important as that is, is as important as their revolutionary conception of what ought to be the relation between Christianity in general, and the Church of England in particular, and the secular order of society.

Hitherto men might well believe that it was the duty of the Church to rebuke and to edify and to instruct men in their duties, but on the whole it had been generally accepted that one of its functions was to give its sanction to the existing order. It is true that many of the Puritans had been in revolt against this idea, but the concern for social justice in the Puritan revolution was on the whole a by-product, which did not produce important results. The primary interests of the Puritan revolution were religious, and its most lasting, beneficial, effects were religious and political. Now the old idea that religion, or the Church, should sanction and sanctify the order of society is not necessarily wrong. Indeed it can be a very fruitful idea, particularly if the conception of social order is made to include social justice. Even if the conception shrinks, as it often did, to the mere idea that religion condemns that disorder which might prevent the maintenance of a stable framework for life, it is still defensible, for after all it is necessary that men should be delivered out of the hands of their enemies to serve God without fear. But the conception can shrink still further and become morally intolerable, particularly if the probable enemies of order are no longer such people as unruly nobles and stout gentlemen but the poor simply because they are poor. Then indeed the conception of the function of religion may be degraded till men think of it as merely something which can save the timid from his fears, the rich man in the enjoyment of his possessions, or even the unjust man in the possession of his spoils. Then indeed, to use a phrase coined by Charles Kingsley in 1848, the Bible will be turned into 'a mere special constable's handbook—an opium dose for keeping beasts of burden patient while they were being overloaded'.[1]

Against this the Christian Socialists protested with great courage. In their view religion, the Church and the Bible existed not to protect, or palliate, what was unjust in the order of society,

---

[1] Raven, *op. cit.*, p. 14.

but to condemn it and to propose a better way; and, in the light of this, they condemned the iron law of competition and tried to substitute for it association and co-operation. They were of course swimming against a still fiercely running tide, their ideas went clean contrary to the accepted orthodoxy of the day. Any impious attack on the law of competition, or on the prevalent view of the limitations of state action, was apt to be received with anger or contempt. Macaulay treated both Southey and Sadler with contempt. As late as 1860, when Ruskin started to produce *Unto This Last* in the *Cornhill Magazine*, the row was so great that the series had to be stopped, and he had the same experience when he tried to produce *Munera Pulveris* in *Fraser's Magazine*. The Christian Socialists also received their meed of abuse, particularly Kingsley, who was the kind of man who naturally drew fire; while his association with Christian Socialism added venom to the miserable persecution of Maurice. Of course all this noise was not only caused by the fact that a fashionable theory was attacked. Its cause came largely from the feeling that these men seemed to want to turn the world upside down, and in the case of Kingsley and Maurice that it was unaccountable and wrong for clergymen of the Church of England to wish to do any such thing.

Nevertheless, they made their point; their view did not simply become tolerated, it became orthodox. Their tradition was of course followed by others who found in the teachings of the Church and the Bible the teachings of a social revolution, indeed of a revolution more drastic than any to which Kingsley or Maurice would have assented. More important, however, than this was the gradual change in the views of almost everyone who gave thought to the problem of the relation of Christianity to the community, so that nowadays it would probably take as much courage as the Christian Socialists originally showed to present the Church as the mere bulwark of what happens to exist.

Of course the Christian Socialists alone were not responsible for this change, the attitude of churchmen in general changed with the general attitude of the time. As the nineteenth century progressed the cause of social reform came to seem more morally urgent and, for that matter, more politically safe, so that fewer and fewer men were content to defend the inequalities of society. Nor had all the prophets who had caused that change of heart prophesied in the Name of the Lord. It would indeed be interesting, and very difficult, to work out the theological

L

position of many of them; to work out, for instance, the relationship to Christianity of Charles Dickens, with his bitter hatred of cruelty yet his inability, at least according to Lord Acton, to know anything 'of sin when it is not crime'. A still more complicated and interesting problem is the origin of that passionate and moral condemnation of social injustice that gives fire and value to the works of Marx, yet does not seem to be justified by the philosophy which he thought he had adopted. But such enquiries are beyond the range of this book. Suffice it to say that there was a profound change in men's attitude to poverty, and that not only was there a comparable revolution in the conception, which many Christians entertained of the function which the Church might perform for society, but that Christians as Christians had pointed to the necessity of change before it was either fashionable or popular so to do; in fact they had played no inconsiderable part in bringing these changes about.

Indeed if one surveys the whole nineteenth-century scene one is struck above all things with the expansive force and the originality of nineteenth-century Christianity. It had been confronted by a situation which was both difficult and dangerous. It had been confronted not simply by a rise in population, but by men and women existing in numbers beyond any figures that had ever existed before. It had been confronted with new and very potent forces in politics and not less in industry and commerce. Yet it had ridden the storm; it had developed new force to meet the new problems. It had covered the country with churches and chapels, and brought many of the new millions within its sphere. It had crossed the seas and started to spread itself over the area which nineteenth-century commerce and exploration opened up, which was little less than the whole inhabitable area of the globe. It had confronted the social problem at home, and some, not all, Christians had seen the way round the ugly reef of the iron law of competition. There had of course been failures and hypocrisy and negligence where there ought to have been the love of God, but taking all together, the Dissenters, the missionaries, the revival of the Church of England, the Catholic revival, the factory reformers and the Christian Socialists the record is very remarkable. But there was one thing nineteenth-century Christianity could not do: it could not control the future. If institutions were to be no longer habits but ideas, it could not ensure that they would be Christian ideas.

For instance it is possible that the remoulding of society which the Christian Socialists demanded has not taken place entirely on lines that they would have desired. This is, of course, partly, no doubt, because they were men of their time. For all their Radicalism many of them retained much of the old picture of society. Charles Kingsley might on an important occasion declare that he was a 'Church of England Parson and a Chartist', but he was also in some ways quite frankly a Tory, a country parson who believed in the gentry and the House of Lords and who, in 1852, believed that the real battle of the time was between 'the Church, the gentlemen, and the workman, against the shopkeepers and the Manchester School'.[1] In *Unto This Last* Ruskin attacked with great bitterness the oppression of the poor and the teachings of the political economists as he understood them, but he also taught the impossibility of equality, and the security of property though he declared that security must also extend to the property of the poor.[2] But the most interesting mind of all was the mind of Maurice. Of the depth and sensitiveness and value of his feelings for the working classes there can be no doubt, but he too still seems to have accepted the social hierarchy of society for he apparently believed that one of the advantages of popular education was to teach 'the poor man that he need not envy and hate the rich man for his superiority to him'.[3] He also believed passionately in the necessity of a union between Church and State,[4] and confronted by those who were in 1870 demanding secular education he believed that, 'It behoves us to maintain our Christian Education; to make it more, not less, distinctly Christian than it has been hitherto'.[5] In politics his ideas fell short of democracy as many understand it, for he declared that: 'I must have Monarchy, Aristocracy and Socialism, or rather Humanity, recognized as necessary elements and conditions of an organic Christian Society',[6] and he could not accept the divine right of the rule of numbers. 'But the sovereignty of the people, in any sense or form, I not only repudiate as at once the silliest and most

---

[1] *Alton Locke*, ed. 1881, Preparatory Memoir by Thomas Hughes, p. 52; *Charles Kingsley: His Letters and Memories of His Life*, edited by his wife, 4th Edition, London 1877, Vol. I, p. 315.

[2] Ruskin, *Unto This Last*, ed. 1900, Essay III, 54, p. 100.

[3] Sermon, 'On Christian Education', preached on the morning of November 20th, 1870, London 1870, p. 10.

[4] Maurice, *Life of Frederick Denison Maurice*, ed. 1884, Vol. II, pp. 8 and 9.

[5] Sermon, November 20th, 1870, p. 9.   [6] *Life, op. cit.*, Vol. II, p. 131.

blasphemous of all contradictions, but I look upon it as the *same* contradiction the same blasphemy in its fullest expansion of which the kings have been guilty.'[1]

Such an attitude was no doubt partly to be explained by the fact that even Maurice was a child of his time. He was also a dreamer of dreams. They were noble dreams and it was well for us that he dreamt them, but it may be that it required harsher forces to conquer reality. Perhaps it is the tension between the ideal and normal reality which may partially account for a certain obscurity in the language of much of his writing, as of a man trying to express things which will not fit into normal phraseology; certainly this tension accounts for his shrinking from the proliferation of societies to agitate this or that practical reform, and from the elaboration of machinery to organize the co-operative movement on a practical basis. 'God's order', said he, 'seems to me more than ever the antagonist of man's systems; Christian Socialism is in my mind the assertion of God's order. . . . Every attempt to hide it under a great machinery, call it Organization of Labour, Central Board, or what you like, I must protest against as hindering the gradual development of what I regard as a divine purpose.'[2] But for any reconstruction of society system was to be necessary, large scale organization was going to be necessary; and it was going to be necessary to enforce the change by means of that great dynamo of political power, the sovereignty of the people.

And there is another point on which the future events were not going to follow the course Maurice desired. Maurice hoped for a society whose order should be an assertion of God's order, and which should accept more fully than did the England he knew the sovereignty of Christ. It is of course an idea that assumes that most people in the country will continue to believe in God, and are prepared to understand what is meant by the sovereignty of someone else than themselves. In Maurice's day it was perhaps not absurd to make such assumptions, though perhaps over-sanguine in him to expect that the results which he desired would spring from them. It was, indeed, because his hopes were of this nature that Maurice desired the continuance of the alliance between the Christian Church and the state, and here he was in

---

[1] *Life, op. cit.*, Vol. I, p. 485. See also F. D. Maurice, *Representation and Education of the People*, London 1866, pp. 201 *ff*.

[2] *Life, op. cit.*, Vol. II, p. 44.

line with ancient tradition. Maurice's views were certainly more radical in their results, and probably more spiritual and more vague in their ideas than the old conceptions about the alliance of Church and state, but they were on many points substantially the same. The Church had always been supposed to be the counterpart of secular power in the spiritual order, and to have authority to instruct secular society in its spiritual duties.

But if for the Church you read the Church of England there had even by Maurice's day been a change. By Maurice's day the position of the Church of England was already equivocal. In 1838 a very intelligent young Churchman, W. E. Gladstone, had written a book to reconcile the old position of the Church of England with the conditions of his time, but as politics developed he himself had virtually to confess that what he had claimed was impracticable. He never produced another theory to take the place of the old one, indeed it may be doubted whether any possible theory, even when produced with that subtlety of which Mr. Gladstone was almost disastrously capable, could have covered the mixture of ancient survival, stubborn habit, and modern political limitation which defined the position of the Church of England in the last half of the nineteenth century.[1] But from all that muddle one fact stands out clearly. Whatever advantages the nation drew, and still draws, from the fact of the establishment of the Church of England, it was no longer likely to accept from that Church instruction which would govern the order of the whole commonwealth.

Nevertheless nineteenth-century England was still a Christian country; only in existing conditions Christianity was inculcated not by one Church which claimed to contain the whole community, to be the whole community in spiritual matters, but by a number of separate bodies, not assisted by the state, claiming only the allegiance of those who were to volunteer to be members of them, and competing with one another. This indeed was the natural result of the variety of conflicting opinions which had developed in nineteenth-century England, and for that matter in nineteenth-century Europe. It was if you like the result of the march of independent intelligence. Yet it is important to realize

[1] On Gladstone's position, see A. R. Vidler, *The Orb and the Cross*, London 1945. This book also contains an extremely interesting introduction to the whole problem.

that this state of affairs probably had certain results on the way religious bodies thought about themselves and about their relationship to the state.

The nineteenth century was remarkable for its renewed emphasis on the doctrine of the Church. Among the Roman Catholics, most noticeably in the Church of England, but also even among the Dissenters, religious teachers dwelt with renewed force on the importance of the Church as a holy and organic body equipped with discipline and particular dogma through which men found salvation. Now this new emphasis was no doubt in part caused by the renewal of old and important theological truths, but that was not its only cause. In a divided, competitive and potentially hostile society it was inevitable that religious societies should close their ranks and emphasize the sanctity and importance of their corporate unity in contrast to the unbelieving world that surrounded them. It was probably so on the Continent where the Church of Rome was at grips with the revolution, it was certainly so in England where even those Dissenters who rejected any High Church doctrine still recognized the importance of a wider and better general organization if they were to compete effectively. It was pre-eminently so in the English Church.

The Oxford movement started in 1833 in direct response to the shocks which the Church had received from the first reformed Parliament, and seemed likely to receive from the Liberal opinion that was massed behind it. In that crisis the Oxford theologians wished to direct men's minds to the doctrine that the Church of England was part of a universal body which had existed before the Reformation, and that therefore it drew its authority rather from the fact that it formed part of the Church of the Apostles than from the territorial and historical accident that it was the Established Church of England, of which position it might be deprived. The very first of the Oxford tracts points the issue and is urgent with a sense of immediate danger. Of course, as is clear from Newman's *Apologia*, a readiness to take up that position had been prepared by much previous study and thought, and the whole ground was prepared for the movement by the Romantic revival, which had nothing to do with the Reform Bill. Certainly also the movement went on to developments infinitely remote from the political crisis. But the conjunction of events is significant, significant of the effects which the new form that society was taking was to have, in all religious bodies, on the conception of what a Christian Church was.

Not that the conception of the Christian Church as a body separated from an indifferent or hostile world was new. Not to go back to the centuries before Constantine such a conception had been inherent in the views of many Puritan sects. Any Church which makes the specialized experience of personal 'conversion' its sole condition of membership must be a body which tends to separate itself off from the bulk of the community. The tendency can even be seen in the Evangelical party with their discrimination between 'vital' Christians and the rest. There is a trivial piece of evidence of this attitude in an advertisement which appeared in *The Times* in 1860 and was copied out for adverse comment by *Punch*. It runs as follows: 'BUTLER WANTED, an experienced middle-aged man, without encumbrances, for a large family, decided in his religious views (Evangelical). No nominal Christian need apply.'[1] But in the past the Church of England had at least been one to which nominal Christians could apply, however many their encumbrances, in fact they were already conceived to be members of it, since the Church was considered to be equally extensive with the community. Now, however, the change in the community was leading even that Church to try to tighten its discipline, consolidate its organization and emphasize the obligations of membership. Of course there were great advantages in this, the advantage of a renewed emphasis on an important portion of Christian doctrine, the advantage of the shedding of the lukewarm, and a reduced estimation of the importance of the social and political alliances which that Church had previously enjoyed. But there may have been disadvantages too. It might possibly lead, to quote F. D. Maurice again, 'To a low view I mean of spiritual blessings, to a habit of regarding them as the property of an exclusive body or of the individual elect; not as treasures like the light and air of which all may partake together: hence to a misunderstanding, contraction, or under-realizing of the truths of God's Absolute, Fatherly love, of the Incarnation, of the Sacrifice for all, which are the great elements of Christianity as the Revelation to mankind and the universe'.[2]

These strictures may or may not be fair, they are certainly

---

[1] *Punch, or the London Charivari*, Vol. 38, p. 91.
[2] *Life, op. cit.*, Vol. II, p. 9.

controversial. But without trying to discuss them it will be a good thing to turn from the effect of this position on the theory of the Church to its effect on the theory of the state. Of course for a Christian Church to have to confront a heretical, indifferent or even actively hostile state was also in no ways new, and it was possible for Christians to render loyalty to such a state when it pursued the purposes for which they conceived it to exist; St. Paul had seen to that. But there must be a difference, under this new competitive system, in the way men look at that state. When the state was the counterpart of the Church in secular affairs men could assume that all men and women in the state shared the same common stock of moral ideas, that their highest spiritual aspirations when relevant could properly direct the action of the state, and that the moral ideas which their Church taught could give form and order to secular society. But in the competitive, sectarian, society many of these feelings are impossible or much reduced. Men know that their highest spiritual aspirations, even their ordinary day to day moral rules, cannot direct the actions and arrangements of secular society, for they are not shared by all the members of secular society. They are confined to members of their particular Church, and secular society becomes in their eyes therefore to be something conducted on a lower plane, and probably for lower ends. Therefore since the highest and best standards are by hypothesis unknown to it, the natural temptation is to come to despise such common moral ideas as secular society does possess and to look upon the secular state as something without much moral order, merely the sphere in which competing bodies of organized opinion operate for their own ends, a thing without form if not void.

It cannot be denied that the feeling that they live in a pagan or indifferent society gives religious people a certain exhilaration, something of the moral exaltation of living in the catacombs without any of the danger. But the condition implied has never been quite true of this country, and if it were true it would be dangerous. There must be some generally accepted ethical code in any community if life as an organized community is to be tolerable or possible. There must for instance be some code so generally accepted that it will control the actions of any normal man towards his neighbour, or his wife, or his children; and the fact that English life has been what it is, and is still what it is proves that some such generally accepted code exists.

Indeed it is not true, and it never has been true, that society in England is a moral void, except in so far as individual Englishmen were instructed by individual religious bodies. There has always been a common Christian tradition in the country, which is not only the sum of the teaching of those bodies, but partly the inheritance of a common Christian past. It may never have been a high enough common factor to achieve Maurice's ideal, but it has never sunk so low to permit those things of which a truly pagan society would be capable. We started the nineteenth century with a very valuable moral capital in the conception of the rule of law, the responsibilities of social position, the sanctity of freedom of speech and opinion, the sanctity of freedom in general, the importance of honesty and a belief in the truth of the Christian religion. The nineteenth century made the observance of some of these traditions more real than they had been before, and to these older traditions the late eighteenth and nineteenth centuries added a new realization of our duty towards primitive and subject peoples, while the nineteenth and twentieth centuries added also a new realization of the moral need so to reorganize society that its order may be just.

To these traditions we of the twentieth century are heirs, and yet it is not quite clear that we are in secure possession of the whole inheritance. In the late nineteenth century, and also in the early twentieth century there were not only important additions to our common moral stock, there was also wastage. It must be remembered that in late nineteenth-century and twentieth-century England the opinions competing for mastery were not all of them Christian opinions. As has been suggested the body of intelligent attack on the Christian faith developed as the nineteenth century progressed till its onset was formidable indeed; but it must be realized that the criticism of Christianity was only part of a wider critical movement that is one of the most remarkable products of that very remarkable century. All through the century men had been learning to try everything, to question everything, to criticise everything, till by the end all accepted institutions and ideas had been brought to the crucible: the old ideas of patriotism, the old ideas about marriage, the institution of private property, accepted forms in poetry, in art and in music. All had been tried and in most of them men had felt that they had detected false metal. The work was done in large part by men and women of great power and integrity. Whatever else may be said of Carlyle and John Stuart Mill, of George Eliot and Ibsen, of Huxley and Marx to name only a few of them, they cannot be accused of lack of ability, and not at all of levity. Nor is there any doubt that much of the work was salutary and healthy. There is no need to deny that there was much that was pretentious or unreal, cruel or corrupt, concealed among the household gods which the men of the nineteenth century had inherited from the past.

Such periodical spring-cleanings are necessary to liberate human thought. But this was an unusually destructive spring-cleaning, with a good many intentional breakages, as more and more people took a hand in the job. As so often happens unfashionable rebellion turned into a fashionable pastime that yielded dividends. In the twentieth century a very profitable line of literary business came to be the attack on a race called first, 'the early Victorians' and then in general the 'Victorians'. Satire on the Victorians came to be part of the usual dreary stock in trade of the ordinary literary hack, but the work was on occasion done with great artistry and skill, as in that remarkable and influential book, Mr. Lytton Strachey's *Eminent Victorians*; and the unscrupulous liberties which Mr. Strachey was able to take with the evidence shows how few effective defenders the great figures of the past still retained.[1] Many of the satirists were of course simply out for fun, others turned to the task with more serious motives but not always with the discriminating knowledge or the sense of historical perspective which alone make historical criticism of any value at all. And as a result of all this activity the impression got abroad that pretty well everything about the men of the last century had been wrong. Their morals had been hypocritical, their literature tedious, their heroes frauds, their womenfolk insipid and their dress absurd: they had bullied their families, repressed their natural appetites and exploited their work people, for underneath all their exploits and over all their aspirations could be scribbled that accusation, to make which costs a man of this century nothing at all in either sympathy or courage, 'they did not feel as we feel about social justice'.

And the disgrace of the Victorians implied disbelief in many of the values they had cherished. It would be extremely interesting

[1] For an exposure of Mr. Strachey's historical methods, see B. M. Allen, *Gordon and the Sudan*, London 1931, pp. 82–101, and F. A. Simpson, *Cambridge Review*, Vol. 65 (December 4th, 1943), p. 120, on Manning.

to work out the history of the decline of those values in various classes of the community, but it would be difficult because apart from such evidence as the divorce statistics or the statistics about Church attendance there would be little firm ground to go upon. Besides in a good many cases the stages of erosion were not easily perceptible. In certain cases there was a definite reversal of values in the life of one individual, or more often a sharp contest of opinion between two generations; but in many more cases there seems to have been a slow surrender, a gradual and progressive disbelief in things which men and women were unwilling to abandon, while they retained an uneasy feeling that somewhere someone had proved them to be incredible or discreditable or absurd. Men no longer talked with such gusto about the inheritance of freedom of which their forefathers had been so proud; patriotism was not lost, in fact in months of peril it flamed up to unexampled heights, but in between wars it became rather ashamed of itself and the country lost its self-confidence to the great disadvantage of the world; thrift and hard work seemed outdated virtues irretrievably mixed up with the capitalist system, and Christianity was relegated to the singing of a few carols at Christmas and the practice of having babies christened and young couples married in Church. In fact in many cases there was no definite rejection of old values, rather the tide of fluid opinion began to set back from the known shore ruled by habit and tradition to flow towards the inane.

But if the old sanctions were to go, the old authorities to disappear, whence would the community draw that common code of morality which it ought to have if it is to continue to be a community? It was a question to which many of the older critics were confident that they had a satisfactory answer. There was a better lawgiver than the God of Moses and Mr. Gladstone. W. K. Clifford, a scientist of the '60s and early '70s, ends a drastic paper on the 'Ethics of Religion' with these sincere and not unmoving words: 'The dim and shadowy outlines of the superhuman deity fade slowly away from before us; and as the mist of his presence floats aside, we perceive with greater and greater clearness the shape of a yet grander and nobler figure—of Him who made all Gods and shall unmake them. From every soul, the face of our father Man looks out upon us with the fire of eternal youth in his eyes, and says, "Before Jehovah was, I am".'[1]

[1] W. K. Clifford, *Lectures and Essays*, London 1879, Vol. II, p. 245.

But as the twentieth century wears on that answer has come to seem a little less hopeful than it used to do. No doubt the question whether man existed before Jehovah is the most important question, but a subsidiary question of some little relevance is the way man has behaved since W. K. Clifford, during which period he has, for instance, reintroduced torture and slavery into Europe. In fact, it may be very tentatively suggested that in general his behaviour has been such that a satisfactory common system of ethics may not be expected with certainty from his unaided imaginings.

But are his imaginings really unaided? A lawgiver ought to make his own laws, but in spite of the grandeur of man is it quite certain that he is his own master? Is it not possible that what he believes to be his own scale of values has really been imposed upon him by the compulsions of the process of evolution, compulsions which might lead some groups of men into very queer actions in the quest for survival? Or may it not be that his actions and desires are dictated by the economic conditions of the society in which he lives? Or the peculiar compulsions of underground psychological forces? These may be difficult questions but it is well to be certain what the answer is to be, for in modern society one thing is certain: it is the increasing over-mastering power of the state, nominally based on that sovereignty of the people, which Maurice called blasphemous. However, when the gods are unmade that word has no meaning.

The modern situation would seem then to be this. The various religious bodies are still very strong, probably stronger than their opponents imagine. There is still a very valuable tradition in the country, probably more valuable than the devout are willing to believe. But religion has certainly lost for the moment the exuberant force that was so important in the history of the nineteenth century, many of the older traditions are for one reason or other discredited or neglected. Even the idea of tradition is one this century does not accept readily.

Therefore the moment has come for taking stock, to see what our traditions have been and to what extent they have been derived from Christianity. It is desirable to do this, not to try to persuade men to believe in Christianity, if they cannot; for after all you can believe in Christianity for one reason only, because you think it is true. But it is desirable to take stock so that people should know where they are. For if this is an age in which we have rejected as guides to tradition the authority that used to be inherent in the older order, then it ought to be an age of conscious decision and not of drift, and you are liable to continue to drift if you do not know where you are and how you got there, or which way you seem to be going.

This stocktaking I have attempted but now that all the lines have converged on the twentieth century there are certain general comments on the whole I would like to make in my last, short, concluding chapter.

X

CONCLUSIONS

'Not without celestial observations can even terrestrial charts be accurately constructed.' S. T. Coleridge, Church and State.

SO the ruins, and survivals, of the different and successive attempts to apply Christianity to English affairs surround us on every side. We still live in part under the protection of the rule of law, we have retained something of our balanced constitution, the remnants of the aristocratic system, with its reinforcement from the public schools, are still with us. In the coronation service we still repeat those solemn rites which teach the bonding of the whole nation together under oath to the protection of justice and the service of Christ. The Church of England, the Protestant Nonconformists, the Oxford Movement and the revived Roman Catholics are all very much alive while we inherit much more than we know from the Evangelical Revival and the Puritan Revolution. And all is set in a medium compounded of national qualities to which it would be difficult to ascribe any historical origin, the sweet English good humour, the foolish English contempt for ideas, and the stubborn English courage which has enabled English troops to struggle to victory from many a scene of near disaster into which the recurrent negligence of the English has led them.

There are many survivals, and their strength is much greater than superficial observers might suppose, but they survive in an altered world. The outward flow of nineteenth-century opinion has had its effects. The destiny of the country can no longer be worked out on the assumption that however much Englishmen may differ they share a common belief in Christianity. Nowadays there are many Englishmen who conscientiously reject Christianity, many more who do not really know what it is that the Christian faith teaches, and others who would like to believe but are gnawed by an uneasy feeling that in some way Christianity has been disproved, and that it is no longer intellectually respectable.

This cuts us off from our past. It cuts us off as a nation from many of the moral assumptions on which our institutions are based. It cuts us off from much of the historical experience and the great literature which can give perspective and depth to our understanding of human behaviour and human personality, a severance which is assisted by the unfortunate modern instinctive belief that what is most valuable in knowledge is an understanding of technical skills and processes, and that remote history and great literature are merely the dead instruments of schoolmasters, or the tedious recreation of exceptional people.

This situation must affect the approach of Christianity, or of the Christian Church, to the modern community. Now Christianity has been related to the secular world in roughly two fashions. There is the institutional relationship, in which Christianity is woven into the whole traditional texture of life and settled institutions, and the representatives of the order of the Christian Church have their unquestioned places in the order of society. And there is the prophetic relationship, in which the Christian Church has stood apart from society, as a body of men and women who were separated by their beliefs from their neighbours, a body whose duty it might well be to testify against the usages of society and if need be to receive persecution. Neither ideal necessarily excludes the other, nor is either ideal necessarily attached to any particular type of Christianity. It is true that, partly as a matter of historic accident, in English history the prophetic approach has often been Puritan and the institutional possibly Catholic, or representing part of the Catholic tradition, to use that very difficult word very loosely. But in a pagan society, however much any Church may claim affinity to the whole tradition of the past, it will be necessary for it to stand aloof from the usages of the present and perhaps to bear witness against them; and in modern England, though both types of relationship survive, for the moment it may well be that the prophetic function must predominate.

There are advantages and disadvantages in this situation. There are obvious advantages for a Church which has been forced by circumstances into the prophetic rôle. Such a Church must be alive, there will be little room in it for the conventional and the torpid. It may be revolutionary. Its members will be led to take nothing for granted but to test all accepted relationships and practices by the touchstone of a lively faith; and it will not be encumbered by irrelevant secular duties and preoccupations. But there will be disadvantages as well. The prophetic situation may lead men to the heresy that Christianity can only be the affair of certain like-minded and unusual people; it may lead to the spiritual heritage of the past being irreverently dissipated by the idiosyncracies of the present and cause grave spiritual loss, even when modern idiosyncracy claims to speak in the name of all that has been truly Christian in bygone ages. And the prophecies of the Church may be morally irresponsible. Since it is probable that the prophets will stand aloof from the community, they may take no count of the certain results which their lessons would have on the order of the community if they were put into effect, and thus they will be confirmed in their spiritual pride by uttering condemnations while they continue to enjoy the protection and the advantages to be derived from the very things they condemn.

But there is no situation without danger, there can be no relationship between the Church and society which is right everywhere, right for everyone, and right for ever. As the course of history unfolds itself, as circumstances change so must the rôle which Christianity performs in society change also. One thing only is permanent, it is human failure. Whatever the relationship between Christianity and society it is certain to be imperfect. The ethics which Christianity teaches are higher than those which ordinary men and women are prepared to practise, its spiritual conceptions more exalted than they are normally willing to reach; and there is no trick of organization or of system which can negative these facts. In fact by so much the more that men attempt to write Christianity into the institutions and habits of their world by so much the more will hypocrisy be increased, and Christianity will be involved in the common failure of all human institutions to live up to their pretensions.

This failure is not new. It has been said that Shakespeare places in the mouths of his characters an expression of that conception of degree, of an ordered community, which seemed so important to the sixteenth century; if so he also causes several of his characters to make passionate protest at the way that order was habitually abused. That feeling appears in the complaints of Hamlet against the world which he was afraid to leave, strangely, for the speaker is a prince and the woes he speaks of are those of subjects. It is urged with magnificent rhetoric in *Measure for*

Measure when Isabella pleads with Angelo for her brother's life. But its most poignant expression is in *Lear*, when misery and madness show the old king shadows on earthly majesty which he never saw in the days of his power and sanity:

> *Poor naked wretches, whereso'er you are,*
> *That bide the pelting of this pitiless storm,*
> *How shall your houseless heads, and unfed sides,*
> *Your loop'd and window'd raggedness, defend you*
> *For seasons such as these? O, I have ta'en*
> *Too little care of this!*

And as his wits crumble he sees clearly the hypocrisy of what human might calls justice, in all its deformity and its respect for persons.

> *Plate sin with gold*
> *And the strong lance of justice hurtless breaks*
> *Arm it in rags, a pigmy's straw doth pierce it.*

The association of Christianity with this repeated failure has led to some of the ugliest ironies of history, the cross glittering in the crown of the cruel king; the crucifix behind the chair of the inquisitor or possibly above his instruments of torture; the words of religion in the mouth of Cromwell as he watched the remnants of the garrison of Drogheda burning alive; or the fat and cynical absentee clergyman living idly on the endowments of piety. But it is not on Christianity alone that such shadows have been cast. From the crimes committed in the name of liberty in the French Revolution to the last travesty of justice or example of ruthless oppression in Eastern Europe the history of modern secular ideals have exhibited from time to time the same unhappy contrasts, the contrast between high pretension and evil performance, between the noble words of man and the ferocity and selfishness of his actions.

But that does not mean that it is better for man to be without ideals, or that it is undesirable for him to try to associate Christianity with his institutions and practices. On the contrary, men with high ideals have on the whole done better than men with low ones, and there is ample evidence that the mixture of Christianity with the institutions of humanity has served to exalt those institutions to ethical standards which otherwise they would not have reached. But it does mean that we may have to change our

M

minds about what we may hope to find in history, that we had best not look to find there any final theory about the nature of the state, or any relationship between society and Christianity which will continue to satisfy indefinitely. Theories that remain untried ideals do not matter, and any theory which has been converted into a living system is likely to be dragged down by the passions and selfishness of mankind, until it becomes something which is rightly attacked by Christians as Christians, who must supplant it by something else. This process, the dialectic or argument of the action of history, may have the result of advancing man's conceptions as his experience discharges this or that system as inadequate. Or perhaps it may not, for history has not been a simple succession of clearly defined easily contrasted abstractions from which the correct theory can be selected, or will in due course emerge. It has been rather a series of dramas in which theories, the personal idiosyncracies of remarkable men, the private appetites of all men and what looks on the face of it to be pure chance have all played their part, dramas tragic in the seriousness of their content and, as was likely from the nature of man, very often tragic in their result.

Whether these dramas are separate plays, or different acts in one great cosmic drama moving to some unseen conclusion we cannot tell. It may not matter very much; since in the eye of eternity what may matter most is not the conclusion of the whole, but the fate of each individual actor, and the conscious existence of many of these has been confined to a very small part in the crowd in one scene. Yet for all this the history of England does seem to have some logic or internal consistency. It seems to embody the hammering out, the development, the betrayal, the re-explanation in terms still inadequate, the extension and at times the contraction of one great moral concept, the concept of freedom. The freedom of Englishmen was held to be the object of the English law, it was the subject of the constitutional struggles of the seventeenth century. It was enforced, if also menaced, by the Puritan, claiming for himself a freedom which he believed to be endorsed by God. The Established Church believed that it protected freedom when it tried to check the forces of superstition and enthusiasm, and acknowledged the rights of human reason; the Dissenter believed that he vindicated it when he attacked the privileges of the Established Church. The manufacturer and the Liberal claimed it against the state in the nineteenth century, and the social reformer and the trade unionist against the manufacturer.

It cannot be said that these men's views on the definition of the concept of freedom have been always clear, or adequate, or consistent, or that their boasts about English freedom have always had as much moral justification as they had confidence; but at least till recent years the emphasis on freedom has been dominant. That fact is significant, and with it must be associated another significant fact, the close connexion in the history of England between the history of freedom and the history of religion. Certainly secular forces and secular motives have played a large part in the struggle. Whatever the source of its philosophy the law was largely secular and the lawyers men of secular mind, the Parliaments were often largely secular in motive and in object, the attack on the corruptions of the old constitution was primarily concerned with secular matters, the French Revolution was secular and indeed potentially anti-Christian, the classical economists were pre-eminently secular and much of the Labour movement has been secular also. Yet all the way through the struggle for freedom, religious motives, men with their minds intent on religion, and religious conceptions have played an important, indeed an essential, part. The sanctity of the law derived partly from the fact that it was the decree of the Great Lawgiver, the fact that the king was under the law was enforced by the fact that he was also under God, his power was in due course successfully challenged in the name of the Law and of God, the power of Parliament was in its turn checked by Puritan soldiers in part, if only in part, because they wished to be free to worship God as they believed He had called them to do, and the same forces faced and ultimately helped to check the power of Parliamentary intolerance after the Restoration. In the eighteenth century it was the teaching of Dissenters and the example of the Puritans that helped to instruct the movement of reform, and in the nineteenth century it was the body of Dissenters that formed the largest section of the Liberal camp. Many of the social reformers did their work explicitly on Christian theories and inspired by Christian motives, while it was such forces as popular Wesleyanism that gave many of the working classes their first chance of independent life and thought.

Now this connexion is not accidental for the conception of freedom and the conceptions of Christianity have one thing in common, an attribution of unique importance to each individual human being and to his own use of his own will. In the concept of freedom, or at least in the English concept of freedom, it has been held to be important that as far as is practicable a man or woman should make his or her own practical choices in life, should not be at the arbitrary disposal of any person or body in authority and should be allowed to decide freely on the great issues of faith and opinion which govern the minds of men. There are great difficulties of course in the operation of this conception. Not only are there the ancient problems raised by those measures of coercion which are necessary to make any orderly life in any community possible or safe, but as the conception of freedom has broadened and has come to include freedom from want and freedom from ignorance, the state has, as we have seen, been forced to take to itself new powers which may seriously infringe the power of the individual to choose his own life and make up his own mind. But in the last resort it is the ultimate principle which matters, and that principle is clear.

Now the same principle is fundamental to all Christianity. In that religion each individual, man or woman or child, is uniquely valuable for no other reason than that he or she is a child of God and his actions and thoughts are valuable because he has a soul to be saved. It is true that no individual can live to himself alone, or work out his salvation alone, but in the last resort his own individual action is uniquely important. There are great difficulties in the working out of this principle, possible difficulties about the relation of the individual human reason to the function of a teaching Church, possible difficulties about the relation between the saving grace of God and the unconverted will of man. But the principle of the unique importance of each human being simply because he is a human being, and of his actions simply because they are his own can stand clear of these questions. It is a principle on which all types of Christianity can join, and a principle which has led Christians to endorse the rights of human beings to secular freedom. When the sponsors of the anti-slavery crusade exhibited pictures of a black man in chains kneeling and pleading "Am I not a man and a brother?", when Shaftesbury wished to rescue the factory children because they were souls for whom Christ died, they emphasized the fact that these people had rights simply because they were human beings. It was the same principle which sent the Roman Catholic priest to the cabin in the Irish bog, or to the cellar dwelling in the English slum.

And it is precisely this principle which is in danger to-day. It is perfectly true that nearly every political creed that is proffered in the market place of the world of to-day claims to be founded on the principle of the inalienable rights of human beings, indeed their adherents normally emphasize and exaggerate the failures of the past and claim that they will protect those rights far better than anyone has ever done before. But it may be questioned whether this principle has the same philosophical endorsement in the view of the universe which very many people, perhaps most people, hold. We come back in earnest to a point that has been raised before. Suppose that a man is simply an ingenious confection of atoms, produced by some as yet unknown chemical process, developed to his present stature by the mysterious force of evolution, suppose that he is set in a universe which knows nothing of his needs and in which supernatural laws and sanctions are unthinkable, what special value can lie in any particular example of the species? What rights can it have, if the word 'right' still means anything at all? Why should you not enslave it to obtain its labour, torment it to extract its secrets, or eliminate it without a moment's hesitation if it is inconvenient? To a statesman with important projects on hand for the ultimate creation of a new and better race, or an improved organization of society, such expedients may seem eminently sensible and practical, and it is significant that several practical statesmen in this modern scientific age have adopted them. Of course it is true that such practices strike many of those who believe in a completely material universe with disgust and horror; but it is difficult to see what principle such people can urge against such expedients except their own personal preference, or what general sanction they can invoke except the threat that it will probably be inconvenient for all if such practices become general. But what does their personal preference matter to any one but themselves? And how effective is that threat going to be, or for that matter has ever been, to men who feel assured that they hold the right end of the sword, or of the machine-gun, in their hands.

But even supposing it is firmly accepted that the individual happiness of all human beings will be the object of the future community, yet still there is something lacking to the ideal of freedom. Happiness and freedom are not convertible terms. For the conception of freedom not only must human beings have an intrinsic value, but so must their free actions, and so must their personal responsibility for their own actions. But what if the conviction becomes established that they are never free agents, and are never to be held to be responsible? If their actions and motives are always conditioned, as the word goes nowadays, by their economic situation, or their heredity, or their psychological make-up, or their physiology, what intrinsic value can their free actions possibly have? Indeed what can it matter what the bulk of them do, so long as they are happy? If they are discontented, or criminal, they are probably so only because they are maladjusted, or misfits and in such cases it will be best to call in the government psychologists, and even perhaps the surgeon and the purveyor of drugs, to recondition them so that they fit more neatly into the niche which society has ready for them. Then indeed they will be more useful and therefore more happy.

But the things which disturb the contented usefulness of men and women most are inconvenient ideas and disturbing information from unofficial sources, therefore the government propagandist will be called in to use on them that science which has made such strides in this century, the science of the manipulation of opinion. He will bend their minds in the right direction, while the government censor will prevent interference from outside, and the government school and youth movement will take charge of the young to see that they are framed on the most useful and satisfactory pattern. Of course all these things may be repugnant to us now, but that is because we retain the belief that it is important for ordinary people to make up their own minds for themselves as far as possible; but that is a belief which requires a special philosophical belief about the nature of the mind and the nature of value to support it.

It may, however, be said that religion has a bad record in the matter of freedom of opinion, and that it is the modern world which has cast the shackles from man's intellect. It is certainly true that the record of the Christian religion is in some ways very bad, as it is also true that it was largely, in England at least, both religious people who in the name of religion broke the government control of men's minds; and religious people who in the name of religion accepted the sanctity of the principle of toleration. But the important thing to remember is that in no century and in no community is the principle of the freedom of opinion ever completely safe, for it runs contrary to two permanent tendencies of the human mind, both of which are apt to work in conjunction. One is the tendency to find that certain opinions are a nuisance, and the other the tendency to believe that they are so perverse and ridiculous that only the very foolish will hold them and only the wilful or the malignant will propagate them. Those tendencies have not deserted us. It still may be very easy for men to decide that a certain range of opinion is bankrupt, ridiculous, disproved, the corrupting product of a past stage of society likely to be anti-social, and that therefore there is no case for giving it opportunity to survive. There has been, and still may be, a problem as to what rights may be permitted to free opinion in a country in which an infallible Church predominates, but there may also be a much more urgent problem as to what rights will be permitted to free opinion in a country dominated by infallible science, or what purports to be infallible science.

All this may seem to be fanciful and speculative, and the German and Russian and Japanese precedents remote and exceptional. Moreover it is certainly true that what actually happens in the world is not decided solely by prevalent theory, or philosophical principle. Unconscious traditions, the unanalysed presumptions of what is read, thought or remembered, the general tone of any society, all play their part in deciding what happens, and still more what shall not happen in any given society. But these things may not only be a protection, they may also be a danger, blinding our eyes to real tendencies and true possibilities. For many people the changing scenery of history has had the illusion of permanence, and they have all been deceived. For instance, we are told that the tendencies which produced the Germany of Hitler were present in the German Empire of the nineteenth century. That may or may not be true, but it is certain that thousands of people who knew the old Germany could not possibly have believed that the new Germany was to be what it was. There is constant historic change, and in its course it is at least possible that principle may triumph over habit, the beliefs of mankind determine the general direction in which its affairs develop. If that is so, it is all important that we should retain the principle by which we have so often been inspired, and which we have so often betrayed, the principle of the unique value of the personality and free actions of each several individual, and, if possible, some sort of philosophy which will give it validity.

That is the issue. All other questions are but details. After all, the all-powerful socialist state will be what we make of it. With this principle we may perhaps refashion for the world the old conception of a law which sovereign states may ratify but may not abrogate; but such a law without the sanction of principle is unlikely to be effective for very long. With this principle to guide us, we may with difficulty find our way through the difficult question of the amount of coercion which is necessary and legitimate to secure an orderly and hopeful life for everyone; without it we may not perceive that any problem exists. Therefore it is important to consider again and again what this principle implies and upon what beliefs it is founded and to consider the way it has affected English affairs in the past, both as a warning and as an encouragement.

But for a Christian this situation presents this serious difficulty. To a Christian this principle seems to depend on a faith which all men cannot now conscientiously share. For him the value of man derives from the fact that he is the child of God, and the sanction behind that value is the law of God. It may be true that other universal religions have in the past taught the same kind of principle, but it is also true that if Christianity goes it is not likely that they will replace it. Now it is no good pretending to believe in God, or even in transcendental values, if you do not believe in them, and as is not always realized by those who talk eloquently if vaguely about the values of Christian civilization, those values depend upon a belief in the Christian faith which not everyone finds himself able to accept. But if this is so there can be no service in disguising the fact from ourselves, we must do the best that we can in the circumstances, and hope that men will be still led to obey a Ruler whom they will not recognize.

However, if the present situation presents difficulties and dangers it also presents a challenge. Indeed, the whole present state of the world and of England presents a challenge which, if it is searching, is also inspiriting. The masks have been plucked off so many things, so many paste-board screens have been torn to shreds, while the fluid forces of the nineteenth century have washed from under our feet so much of the dead support of habit. The education which has been so widely extended has, it may be hoped, rendered many minds open to new ideas, and to many people in the present state of England any coherent version of Christianity may well come as a very new idea indeed. The challenge is both moral and intellectual, for Christians must not only, as they are often told, be worthy of their faith, but, as they are not so often told, they must understand it and be ready to explain it; all of which is as it should be, since intellect is the creation of God and the proper instrument of the free man. But whatever the challenge it is urgent and not to be avoided; for the future of the world may lie in our hands, if it is true that the safety and freedom of man lies only in the service of God.

INDEX